Establishing Educational and Economic Equity

Establishing Educational and Economic Equity

By
Dr. Lisa R. Washington
Jeremiah N. Harris

For those who never realized how productive their lives could have been and still can become~
We dedicate this book to you.

Table of Contents

Introduction

Educational and Economic Equity are a set of fundamental beliefs which derive from the very fiber of the "American Dream." These beliefs are relative to the personal and financial goals we set for ourselves on our philosophical journey in life. Similar to our profound spiritual beliefs in God, we have another series of beliefs stemming from mankind's desire to achieve through purpose. The American Dream is the concept most Americans, especially Black Americans believe in wholeheartedly in spite of the social injustices we have experienced in this country. Even though there will always be obstacles in our path, if we work hard enough and believe in ourselves and in our abilities as human beings, we will achieve great heights in this world. The idea of attaining academic achievement in grade school and in college, establishing a professional career, becoming a homeowner, raising a family, and acquiring financial security and freedom are the common threads people associate with the philosophical American Dream.

Over the years, human ideals of obtaining that dream may have varied in approach, but the overarching desire to reach that pivotal moment in one's life has not changed. We all have an innate yearning to achieve in all aspects of our lives. We want to have a good education, earn a good income, and be able to afford all the luxuries in life for ourselves and for our families. Like most things, freedom is not free, and neither is the American Dream. If we want to obtain educational and economic equity, we must understand that it comes with a price. The price is our intent in starting the task, and our internal motivation which is our willingness to complete the job. This is what drives most Americans by prompting us to excel to our fullest potential. As Black Americans this concept remains a constant in our life journey because the pursuit of life, liberty, and happiness is a goal we must accomplish as a race.

With that being said, in life, we are confronted with many decisions and opportunities which impact our lives as individuals, citizens, students, parents and as professionals. Each time we think about our lives we wonder if the decisions we have made are beneficial to us and our families. We also think about the vast opportunities we were given in life and question if we made the best of those moments by determining whether or not we allowed ourselves to excel and become productive members of society. It is a given that each of us reflects on the past with an open mind and a clear perspective.

Knowing that our actions impact our future, we often wonder if it is possible for us to obtain educational and economic equity. This relates to our ability to gain the necessary academic skills we need for college and the workforce, and the opportunity to establish ourselves financially. We also ponder on our personal and professional achievements we accomplished over the years wondering about the significance of those deeds and successes. We question ourselves by asking, "What was the purpose?" Was it an act of self-exploitation or were we just exercising our ability to act accordingly to societal norms? Did we move fast enough, or did we procrastinate for far too long and lose valuable time?

This leads us to evaluate our current state of being in the world by asking, "Did I make the right decision with my life, or did I make a serious mistake?" Reflecting on our place and position in society is the starting point for self-analysis. As Black Americans, we often wonder about our God given rights, purposes, and responsibilities in life. Why were we placed in this world? What is our purpose? These questions may seem futile but they are relevant as it applies to who we are as human beings and why we walk this earth.

For me, these questions have always been at the forefront of my mind. I often find myself wondering if I missed something along the way on my educational and professional journey, and if so, what did I miss? Would knowing what I overlooked in my life alter my current circumstance or not? One thing I do know is that there has to be more to life than just paying taxes, going to jury duty, working a 9 to 5, and obeying the law. Knowing that there are basic rights afforded to all citizens such as freedom of speech, the right to a fair and public trial, the right to due process of law, having the right to vote, and having the right to worship freely is just an inkling of what we as Black Americans are entitled to as citizens of this great land.

It is our divine right to excel as scholars and students of academia in our pursuit of professional and financial growth. We desire the ability to cultivate our minds with worldly experiences from other cultures and localities. This requires us to indulge in the pursuit of individual happiness afforded to all men willing to strive towards an internal goal driven by sheer will. In that regard, one must instill within him or herself a sense of self-awareness and self-confidence in order to shift towards the direction of self-identification and self-gratification for finding one's true purpose in life.

As Black Americans we can develop this sense of self through the process of learning about our personal goals towards establishing a strong family foundation, striving towards intellectual advancement, obtaining homeownership, enhancing our financial security and personal wealth, building effective social networking relationships with other professionals, renewing our lives, and creating a new vision for the Black race by placing emphasis on education and economic equity by using our professional titles and career platforms to increase our productivity levels as a group.

From a parental perspective, parents play an essential part in helping their children reach their full potential in this world. I believe that children are incapable of producing insight into their unique potential without the assistance and guidance from their parents. In that respect, the mother and the father represent the cornerstone of emotional development and physical strength in the eyes of the child. Children idealize both of their parents as iconic pillars of emotional stability and financial security within the household. Having a strong and positive parental figure is essential to child development.

Since both parents represent an important aspect of the social and emotional growth of the child, they are equally viewed as the instructor of life. The mother and the father both are responsible for modeling the process for showing children how to direct and channel their behaviors in a positive way when dealing with conflict. Moreover, both parents are equally responsible for molding the child into a productive and competent member of society. This includes the action of the parents for teaching their child the necessities of life in regards to self-care, self-value, self-esteem, and self-preservation.

However, because things do not always work according to our plans, it is imperative that we embrace the concept of "Educational and Economic Equity" as we consider effective and efficient ways to establish professional and financial freedom and success outcomes for our own families in the year 2020 and beyond. This is not a new concept, but an urgent one to contemplate when considering your child's future and your family legacy moving forward. Educational equity refers to the measure of achievement, fairness, and opportunity in the educational process.

In that, we examine how our children are being taught in the public education sector. Knowing that education is supposed to focus on the whole child, we focus on the three main sectors of education which are the formal, informal, and spiritual aspects of the education process. Then, we ask ourselves, "How are our students being socialized and humanized in these educational settings?" We also wonder if the learning environment itself is functional enough to help our children maintain and establish lifelong learning skills needed to adapt and excel in an evolving and changing society.

When considering the idea of "Economic Equity," we must also reflect on our history in American society. We know that economic equity relates to fairness in economics, and that Blacks have received disproportionate amounts of resources in reference to homeownership, equitable career paying jobs, and financial wealth compared to white Americans. Therefore, the questions which emerge in our minds regarding economic equity are based on social injustice, racism, discrimination, and alienation as a human race. On the other hand, Black Americans have been working tirelessly for over a century to achieve the goals we aspire to as a race of capable, competent, creative, brilliant, and resilient men and women. We know that we have the power to transform our lives in our own favor.

Furthermore, we understand that reaching any level of success in our lives requires dedication and purpose. In order to acquire any level of success, we may have to travel down the road of failure once more, but we will trudge through that dark path towards the bright, burning light of our new future. Like everything in life, we understand that obtaining educational and economic equity is a process which takes time and effort. The reality is that each of us has a chance to become the best person we can in this world through hard work, determination, and good work ethic.

CHAPTER 1:
Family Foundation and Societal Influences

Creating a purposeful and meaningful family foundation is essential to the goal of obtaining educational and economic equity. Someone once said to me "Blood don't make you family." In my younger years that statement would have very little meaning to me. As I've grown and experienced life and learned from the experiences of others, I see this as a profound statement. It reveals the foundation of the troubles that we as a community continue to face. A structured family system is composed of all the pieces needed to allow us to live and thrive in society. So why are Black boys and girls so far behind in the race for equality? Some of the answers to that question are contained in the word "family" itself.

Ideally, a strong family is the foundation for developing a commonwealth system for future generations to come. This means that a well-built family structure generates and produces a wealth of intellectual, competent, diligent, and capable members within its community. Its infrastructure is generally built to last by creating a family legacy of assertive individuals. Positive and loving relationships between mother and father and parent and child are essential factors of this type of family unit. In their study, Feinberg, Jones, Kan and Goslin (2010) assert how, "...Family Foundations may have a positive impact on multiple important domains of parent, child, and family well-being" (p. 540). This can possibly benefit the long-term trajectory of a child's social and emotional health as well as his or her mental stability. But, a negative mindset constructed within the home environment can attribute to the child becoming a behavior problem. According to Blair and Diamond (2008), when children are given misinformation and not being properly taught in the home, multiple issues arise that will negatively impact them in grade school such as, "...problems with self-regulation, particularly problems with following directions and controlling attention as the main cause of children's lack of school readiness" (p. 899). This tends to cause high levels of frustration and academic incompetency for the child. With that in mind, it is pertinent and crucial for Black mothers and fathers to demonstrate positive and effective levels of parenting within the household.

Parents who manifest ineffective and dysfunctional measures of parenting risk creating a home environment where their children internalize those behaviors and view those actions as accepted norms. As parents, we have to teach our children how to self-regulate their own behaviors, so they can demonstrate positive and effective socialization competencies. This is fundamental because the behaviors taught in the home later transcend into the school environment. Children who are taught to self-regulate are least likely to exhibit behavior problems. As a result, these children become more academically competent in the learning community.

Therefore, if the foundation of family is not truly established, we are starting off in the race with lead shoes, and who could expect to finish a race in anything other than last place under those circumstances. There is a need for the Black race to extend the concept of family beyond our bloodline to actually force a change. We also have to come to understand that some family members will be left behind, just as Harriet Tubman had to leave slaves who were not aware they were slaves. Building a strong foundation of like minded souls reaching for the same stars, looking for true understanding of self, and controlling their own financial destinies is at the forefront of rebuilding the Black community. We have to, in some way, build our own nation within this so-called great nation, to actually produce at the level we are fully capable of.

Family Bedrock

In retrospect, we know that family is the "bedrock" which can either lead to individual success or failure. Metaphorically, the bedrock can be extremely solid when referring to a strong family unit, or it can be broken up like a dysfunctional learning environment. The question we are confronted with as a race is, "How do we create a foundation based on love, respect, and purpose?" The difference between a functional family unit and a dysfunctional family unit is contained in the root meaning of the word. For instance, the prefix "dys" means bad, abnormal, difficult or impaired opposed to "funct" which means operational.

If a child is being raised in a dysfunctional home environment the probability of academic and financial success begins to narrow. Whereas being raised in a functional home environment can elevate someone's chances of obtaining future success. There is an iconic saying, "Don't be a product of your environment, make your environment a product of you." Pondering on that intuitive thought, we envision how so many young Black boys and girls continue to be consumed by the negative aspects of life and wonder what can be done to gear them on the right path to social, emotional, academic, and economic productivity.

In response to the question, "Why are so many Black boys and girls so far behind in the race for equality?," one answer to this question is the lack of direction and assertiveness. Boys and girls who do have enough positive parental support rarely interact with others in a respectful and intellectual manner. Instead, these children often appear verbally and physically disruptive in the natural environment while during things such as riding public transportation, sitting in a classroom, frequenting a movie theatre, or shopping at a local mall. If these boys and girls are not assertive, they are not demonstrating evidence of the internal motivation skills they need to excel in life. Another reason for their lack of persistence on the road to equality stems from the choices they make along the way.

Again, this goes back to the concept of the family foundation that is the initial, most important, significant, vital, and chief aspect of a child's learning. It is no surprise that the experiences a child encounters within the family culture can affect how he or she evolves as an individual. Furthermore, those home experiences dictate the choices the child makes because our family is where we derive the majority of our learning behaviors. After all, learning is a taught action and children often internalize what they are taught at home. Without effective and purposeful family direction a child can get lost in the world and make some damaging decisions that will adversely affect him or her in the long run.

Community Involvement

Subsequently, the initiative for placing the Black youth on the road to success will require the assistance and participation of the entire community. This is not by any means an isolated process. The journey of the Black youth begins once he or she receives the seeds of life from home. Eventually, those seeds begin to take root in the streets which stems outside the walls of the home environment. From there, the branches begin to extend towards two different paths. One is a road less traveled and the other is a road often traveled, depending on the socioeconomic boundaries of the community in which the child is being raised.

On this sometimes adversarial journey, the Black male and female youth begin to forge relationships with others where conflict and opposition may arise. Most of the time, the youth tries to de-escalate the situation by taking matters into his or her own hands. Additionally, the Black youth often avoids informing the family about the conflicts he or she has encountered in the real-world, which in turn creates a personal crisis that overwhelms him or her and alters the trajectory of his or her academic journey. This becomes a symbolic boulder on the path to success.

Consequently, Black youths seem to run into three essential roadblocks in their young lives including: (1) they have so many obstacles to overcome; (2) they often have difficulty differentiating between what priorities are essential aspects leading towards their future goals versus priorities that are insignificant and have no purpose in their journey in life, (3) and as a consequence, those distractions along the road hinder their journey and disrupts their future goals. Organizations like Run My City, 100 Black Men of America, The National Black MBA Association, and The National Urban League are positive and influential community programs with the sole purpose of uplifting and mentoring the Black youth by instilling within them the principles of economic empowerment, equity, and social justice.

When I was a child, recreation centers were commonplace and a common practice in my neighborhood. These facilities provided Black youths with a positive and safe environment to play and learn about different sports, discover healthy exercise routines and diet regimens, learn how to cook and sew through home economics, and offered youth both swimming and dance lessons for free (This promotes individualized productivity outcomes). The organizations who ran those facilities were professional, trustworthy, and dedicated agencies. Run My City is an independent community based organization created by Devin Thomas and Jeremiah Harris. Run My City is a coalition that aspires to educate members in urban communities through action and deeds. According to its founders, Run My City is more than just a brand, it is a family. This agency has helped many Black youths by promoting community awareness, social justice, and economic empowerment through a multitude of strategies.

Building community involvement requires community commitment. Like Run My City, 100 Black Men of America is committed to helping Black youths strive and excel in life. This organization gives Black youths something to commit to and build up to as they move towards adulthood. Historically, 100 Black Men of America have been supporting Black communities for the past 57 years. This organization is known for educating and empowering Black children and teens by providing program resources such as mentoring, education, health and wellness, and economic development. Today, this organization of Black men is still committed to its vision and mission of fostering the quality of life and economic opportunities for Black children across America by teaching them how to advance themselves academically, socially, and economically.

Besides Run My City and 100 Black Men of America, The National Black MBA Association is another community based agency whose intent is to provide support to Black youths. The National Black MBA Association is a non-profit organization that has been assisting the Black youth since the 1970s in becoming productive members of society. This particular confederation of Black men has improved the lives of thousands of Black youths living in urban neighborhoods. This organization is based on three core values which are learn, connect, and grow. Members of The National Black MBA Association teach Black youths the skills they need to improve their intellectual knowledge. This consortium is also firm in connecting with Black youths by creating positive and effective relationships with youths and their families. Moreover, The National Black MBA Association is known for helping its members grow both personally and professionally.

The National Urban League is also known for its contributions towards educational and economic equity in Black communities is essential to productive education growth outcomes. The National Urban League is a historic civil rights organization, established in 1910. Their sole purpose is to uplift and empower members of marginalized and underserved communities through educational and economic advancement. This federation of Black men provides educational opportunities to youths, provides people with professional training for career paying jobs, and creates pathways to prosperity through homeownership programs. The overall mission and vision of The National Urban League is to empower communities and change lives.

Once these outside entities begin to intervene in the lives of Black boys and girls the probability of individual success and productivity for these youths begin to elevate. Multiply that by the number of students housed within a single school system. That becomes a life changing event. Unfortunately, many of our Black boys and girls do not have positive role models in the home, and their only option is to seek acceptance and direction from people outside of the home who may or may not have their best interest at heart. Luckily, organizations like Run My City, 100 Black Men of America, The National MBA Association, and The National Urban League have been faithfully committed in their efforts to cultivate and improve the lives of Black youths and other marginalized groups collectively over the past fifty years. Each of these organizations are stationed in multiple cities across America. Thanks to their unwavering commitment to Black communities and youths, progress is being made in the lives of so many individuals who have an internal need to overcome the adversities which continue to plague their neighborhoods and defraud them of their dreams.

The Race for Equality

Moving forward, we know that the race for equality is a serious matter for many Black Americans. This is not a journey or topic that Blacks take lightly. Even though this is 2020, the experiences and challenges which the Black race were exposed to during the days of slavery and even during the Civil Rights Movement continue to plague us as a people. These events have a way of emerging from the past and creeping into our daily lives. In the essay *Notes of A Native Son* it states that, "The making of an American begins at the point where he himself rejects all other ties, any other history, and himself adopts the venture of his adopted land" (Baldwin, 1984, p. 23). With that, we are the change agents in our own life. We are the rulers of our destiny and this lifelong journey.

Today, the tides are turning and Blacks are beginning to internalize the idea that in order to redirect the path of our family and create a legacy for our children, we must take control of our lives. James Baldwin's advice about rejecting all the ties that bind us epitomizes our pursuit for educational and economic equity, especially considering those unhealthy and unproductive ties which lead to failure. For instance, if a family member is holding you back by causing you unnecessary emotional and mental stress, break the tie. If a family member is too dependent on you for their monetary needs, break the tie. If a family member refuses to improve his or her circumstance by going to college or getting a job after you have provided a plethora of spiritual, motivational, and financial support, break the tie. Remember, "Blood don't make you family" it is just a biological relationship between descendents from the same bloodline.

Like a heavy chain, a negative tie can break the human spirit and suffocate the life out of a child, but a positive tie can allow a child to flourish in the world and reach his or her true potential and ultimate goals in life. Throughout the course of American history, Blacks are viewed as nonhuman, uneducated, useless, and unproductive beings. This is a misnomer and a false narrative we have since rejected. From Harriet Tubman to Barack Obama, we see that this is just an illusion racist white America portrayed to us in public through use of Jim Crow Laws and on the Golden Screen in movies such as *Gone with the Wind, To Kill a Mockingbird, Birth of a Nation,* and *the Dead Presidents.*

Racial stereotypes and racial depictions of Black Americans remain the cornerstone of hate, social injustice, and oppression, which permeates into our families and communities by labeling us as unworthy and insignificant people. This is a farce and a tactic of mind manipulation which consumes so many of our Black family units. Do not allow yourselves to be labeled. Do not allow any race to classify your worth and ability. Break away from those historically biased characterizations and become anew. It is time for us as a people to adopt the idea that we cultivated, erected, and advanced this country to its socioeconomic existence on the worldwide stage. That is the history we must instill within our families.

Black mothers and Black fathers, we must rise to the occasion. It is our duty and responsibility to assist our children along their path in life. Black mothers and fathers must have the fortitude to advance themselves and their children on the road to success. Remember that the pursuit of happiness will remain an illusion unless we put weight to it. In order to accomplish our dreams and attain true happiness in all aspects of our lives, we as a people must embrace the concept of creating a strong family foundation built on work ethic, love, respect, and pride that is always based on principle and purpose. We know that excelling in life is not something the Black child can do alone. Support and direction from his or her family is essential because it takes a village to raise a child.

Knowing Your History

Do you know who you are, and where you and your forefathers come from? Are you in a position to answer that question fully as a capable and knowledgeable human being? If you do not know the answers to the previous questions, this explains why so many of our Black boys and girls continue to fall behind on the road to obtaining educational and economic equity and equality. In the movie *Malcolm X,* director Spike Lee confirms this idea by suggesting that Black Americans are not fully aware of their Black heritage, or their contributions to American society. Watching this film, one realizes that the social injustices Blacks have experienced in America will always have a profound effect on us as a people. This is not me solely reflecting on a box office film. This is me reflecting on real life as a Black American and specifically as a Black woman.

As I consider the speeches in the film, "*Malcolm X,*" I can acknowledge that those were the words of Malcolm X having previously read the *Autobiography of Malcolm X* as told by Alex Haley. Just as Spike Lee conducted research to develop the film, *Malcolm X,* we as a race must research our own history. Do not take at face value what another race dictates as being our true history as a people. Reject those unflattering narratives and help to create our own chronicles regarding our race. We must fully embrace the idea that we are a race which stems from Kings and Queens and from greatness. We are also a race that has produced, designed, manufactured, and invented the majority of the technology this country has been utilizing for centuries, and are descendants of the Black men and women responsible for those masterpieces. Ironically, American history vaguely reflects on the contributions the Black race has instituted in this great country saving their acknowledgements only for Black History Month, but the following is a short list of several of our talented and most influential Black inventors, mathematicians, and scientists from the past and those of the present:

1. Lewis Latimer (1848-1928): Inventor and Draftsman- major development of carbon filament patent for a lamp

2. George Washington Carver (1860-1943): Inventor, Scientist and Botanist- major developments prevention of soil depletion

3. Garrett Morgan (1877-1963): Inventor of the traffic light and gas mask

4. Charles Drew (1904-1950): Physician and Medical Researcher major development was the blood bank

5. Katherine Johnson (1918-2020): Mathematician- major developments NASA aeronautics and space program

6. Otis Boykin (1920-1982): Inventor- major developments IBM computer and the pacemaker

7. Marie Bran Britton Brown (1922-1999): Inventor- major developments closed-circuit television security

8. Jesse Earnest Wilkins Jr., (1923-2011): Mathematician- major developments mathematical models to explain gamma radiation

9. Dr. Shirley Jackson (1946-present): Theoretical Physicist major developments- the touch tone telephone, caller ID, and fiber-optic cable

10. Philip Emeagwalie (1954-present): Scientist- major development world's fastest computer

This is just a fraction of the names of Black Americans who have greatly contributed to the socioeconomic, health, and technological advancements of the United States of America. There are many more historical figures to be discovered. I challenge you to make that quest. This is a call to not allow the fallacies of life to define who we are as a people, because we are much greater than the past and better than the future. But, having an awareness of one's cultural and ethnic background is synonymous to knowing and understanding one's heritage.

The Decline of the Black Family Unit

Our true Black history has always been based on family values, integrity, and culture. There is a time I recall from my own childhood memory when my neighbors on Woodhaven Avenue acted as surrogate parents to all the children in the neighborhood. I remember feeling safe and trusting my neighbors' intentions regarding my protection and well-being. One specific incident involved my neighbor, Mr. Walker. One day I and the other kids who lived in the neighborhood were out after curfew. Mr. Walker told us to go inside because it was too late for children to be out in the streets. Someone said something disrespectful, refusing to go in the house. Mr. Walker took off his belt and chased us all into our homes. His actions were protective, innocent and greatly appreciated.

In my opinion, this constitutes an example of community engagement by having the best interest of your community members at heart. You don't see that anymore. There is definitely less community involvement and activism taking place in 2020 compared to my experiences as a child growing up in the inner city of Baltimore. This is why I am as skeptical regarding white America's illustrations of us as a race. Their views are often tainted with blatant cynicism. Furthermore, the negative depictions of Blacks in history books are not a real representation of our great race. Racist white America indulges in the ideals of Black servitude. As depicted in the 2020 film, *Antebellum,* if they could turn back time, they would. The old Negro experiences with oppression are something they admire dearly. Those are the historic narratives used to deflect from the vast contributions Blacks have accomplished in the past, and those contributions and successes we continue to make presently.

It is not until the influx of drugs being funneled in the Black community that we began to see a drastic decline in the Black family unit. This is an episode of B.C. versus A.C. meaning before crack cocaine and after crack cocaine. Once these drugs seeped into the Black community either the Black fathers were selling the drugs or getting arrested with extensive jail time, or family members were getting hooked on drugs and became codependent substance abusers. This is the straw that broke the camel's back and a contributing factor to the decline of the Black family. Even though the foundation for a productive existence starts with family and community, external factors like drug usage, racism, and social injustice can have a crippling effect on the Black psyche.

In the dictionary and in English Literature, the word "black" has been attached to a series of negative concepts and expressions, opposed to the word "white" which is usually referred to from a positive perspective. In that regard, colors have often been used in literature to express character feelings and story events based on real-life scenarios. The phrase, if you are black step back, but if you are white take flight exert a type of racial undertone as does the following representations of the two colors. In reference to the colors white and black, "white" is referred to positively as calmness, peace, purity, honesty, good, and clean. Whereas the color "black" is associated with negative connotations such as darkness, fear, death, evil, aggression, dirty, and cruelty.

But in reality, the color black represents something more relative and unique. Black represents strength, rebellion, mystery, authority, elegance, sophistication and power. Using something as irrelevant and basic as a selection of colors in a crayon box to elicit an act of oppression is manipulative to say the least. Inequality presents itself in various forms, it emerges from multiple outlets in society, and it comes at different times throughout the course of history. It also continues to be based on the premise of mind trickery by using social and political influences to manipulate the Black race.

Unfortunately, the Black community has been brainwashed so much over the course of history that to receive a loaf of bread and a box of government cheese has been viewed as progress. These underhanded and deceptive tactics have placed Blacks living in urban communities in an institutionalized state. Within these communities, Blacks continue to wait on "the white man" for direction for him and his family instead of digging deep within himself to obtain the guidance and direction he needs to become productive. Instead, he continues to live a counterproductive life based on "the white man's" vision of him.

When all is said and done, the new Black History will be reflective of our efforts as a race of people to redirect the path in which the past has placed us on. Do we know who we are as a people? Can we ascertain what issues we face in our communities? Knowing that we were all born with faith in our innocence as a newborn, why would we sentence ourselves to a failed belief system imposed upon us by a group that despises our very existence? In the light of day, can we see what we are dealing with in reference to racial inequality? Do we understand that we have a broken family system that must be repaired? We must focus on what is relevant in meeting the needs of our people and ending centuries of oppression which continues to negatively impact the Black race by presenting us with failed systems that contain no power, and can destroy our very existence. We as the Black race not only have to live we must survive.

Within the Black race, the children only are going to be as good as the parents. There are so many parents who aim to get their kids where they need to be. Their mindset is that our Black children and grandchildren can earn more than we ever did because exposing them to their Black heritage will help them learn and grow as American citizens. Even though we as parents might not know the entire true history of our race, we can educate our families with the knowledge we do possess. In life, there is always a starting point. It is clear that the truth shall definitely set one free. Whenever we fall in life, we should rise up and try again and again until we succeed. Decades ago we faltered as a race from drug usage, excessive incarceration rates, and absence of the father figure within the household.

Considering how those negative decisions and choices can taint and sabotage the Black family unit provokes a sense of awareness regarding action versus outcome. Raising a family requires great sacrifice, and the contribution of positive direction from both parents. Children today have the right to live within a functional home environment free of drama and danger. As parents, we must reiterate to them the behaviors we expect them to demonstrate in society and at home by modeling those same positive behaviors as adults. This is because some things in life cannot be taken for granted. Children continue to idolize their parents and replicate their actions. They often do what they see, and ignore what they are told because a parent's actions speak louder than their words. This is a result of children being curious in nature when they notice behaviors being acceptable and normative.

Therefore, if the kings of men, being the Black men, do what they need to do for building the foundation of the Black race, families would be unified and communities would rise to greatness. Yet again, the idea of not knowing who you are and where you come from will always be a defeating factor in the Black race. However, we cannot allow this drawback to prevent us from progressing forward in the world. This reminds me of one of Maya Angelou's famous quotes that says, *"There is no greater agony than bearing an untold story inside you."* Her words have relevance even today when we ponder on our family and cultural heritage. Not knowing the true story of your race is a mystery, but not trying to bring the story to light will become our greatest tragedy.

Knowing your history as an African living in America, as a Moor living in the United States of America, or as an Israelite living on this unholy plane, I would ask the question, just who are we as a whole? It would seem that Black people are clueless regarding the concept of self and that of a race of people. I use the term Black people to give a general understanding of who I am speaking to. It is my belief that not having a standard identity is another key entity that leaves us in a place of confusion, and allows us to make very little if not any progress towards our true liberation.

We can motivate ourselves to become whatever we want. However, the facts remain the same. We will continue to be killed by white cops more than any other race or ethnic group, if we continue to be on the bottom of the totem pole. When it comes to things like economic power and political influences, we lag way behind other races as a group. Being creators and getting equitable credit for it is something Blacks need to strive towards, especially in the educational areas of science and mathematics. As a race, we are constantly being evaluated by someone else's standards that do not reflect our living conditions or lifestyles.

Therefore, as a Black youth, Why should I compose a paper about *The Great Gatsby* or create an account portfolio of some self-made multi-million dollar business with very little accounting training or experience. It would be far more useful if my writing instructor allowed me to write about a novel that focused on a dope fiend struggle to kick his habit or a drug dealer living a double life and being challenged by his moral conscience. That, in my opinion, would be a more realistic and productive use of my time and energy. Why are Blacks always expected to study and learn about the history of the white race, and prevented from learning about their own culture and experiences as a people? This is a question that has haunted me during my adolescence as a Black youth, and a concept I continue to reflect on as a Black man. Instead of focusing on the history and culture of another race, we need to redirect our attention towards our own race. This is essential since our value system is so fragmented.

Restoring Family Values

There is a deteriorating relationship between children and their parents, especially in the Black community. This is an issue that needs our immediate attention. Children are rebelling against their parents and there is an absence of communication in the home. In an attempt to avoid negative confrontations, parents and children ignore each other as if the other does not exist. Some would blame this issue on societal influences while others may attribute the breakdown to the lack of parental supervision. Whatever the case, this is a serious matter which must be resolved in order to save the Black youth. For the Black race, restoring our family values will create a healthy, nurturing, and productive community of effective and efficient young men and women. When it comes to the restoration of the family unit, this is a major turning point in our journey as a race.

In our pursuit to restore family values in the Black community, we are not attempting to demoralize our own human value, but we are investing in our children's future. This is not about taking on the persona of other cultures. It is about improving the infrastructure of our communities and restoring family values. Therefore, we must set a precedent which encapsulates the very essence of the Black culture to its most moral, ethical, and productive state of existence. For many Blacks living in urban America, the ghetto is a state of mind for some, and a way of life for others. These are mental and physical constructs which have developed over the course of several decades, and it may take that long to deconstruct those ideals to improve the livelihood and family structure of our race. In that, we must transform our moral contradictions of self by doing what is right and good for our own communities.

Basically, Black lives are devalued in America because of societal influences. This is due to an imbalance in the employment ratio, a disproportion in homeownership, inconsistency in education outcomes, disparities in income differentials, and an ingrained prejudice which has been breeding in this country for over a century. That being the case, it is up to us as Black Americans to decide on the path we take to guarantee productivity outcomes for our youth moving forward in 2020 and beyond, and our intentions as a race to improve the family infrastructure in urban communities. By no means is this a fad or a brief novelty. This is a movement to improve the current state of Black people living in America because Black Lives Matter!

Hence, the road to restoring the Black family values is paved with a series of remnants of the past. We know that the concept of the road refers to decisions that have to be made, so it is understandable that this is a journey which requires our full and undivided attention. On that account, we must keep in mind that the loving affection and the spiritual and parental guidance a child receives from home can create a firm foundation leading to future productivity outcomes. These are the elements that build strong family ties and positive long term relationships between parent and child which are reflective of basic family values such as knowing right from wrong, spending quality time together as a family, learning from one's mistakes, thinking before one reacts, and always demonstrating honesty and integrity. Each of these examples help contribute to the restoration of the Black family unit.

Building Strong Communities

Within the urban community, there are many Black families living well below the poverty line. These families are housed in devastating environments where poverty, drugs, alcoholism, and poor living conditions are prevalent. This is due to unemployment, lack of opportunities, lack of education, or just one's lack of trying. Whenever someone manages to escape from this type of environment and succeed, that person is coined as being *"A diamond in the rough"* because it is a rare instance when someone is able to elevate themselves from the confines of an imprisoned state of confinement, especially when harsh and dangerous conditions seem insurmountable.

I remember when I was eight years old riding my bike around the neighborhood thinking to myself, "There has to be something better than this, a place more beautiful than this, somewhere to call home." Through my innocent eyes as a child, my future was always the one thing I pondered about day and night. When I reflect on the lives of Black families and youths living in the inner city of Baltimore, I pray for their well-being and success. As an educator, I am fully aware of the value of an education, and how obtaining academic success can change and enhance the life of the average human being.

Even though there are multiple issues infesting and plaguing Black neighborhoods like drugs, poverty, unemployment, and poor housing conditions, we know that we have a collective goal and obligation as a community to restore and rebuild those areas. Rapper Killer Mike made a powerful statement during the Black Lives Matter movement when he said, "It is your duty to fortify your own house, so that you may be a house of refuge in time of organization. And now is the time to plot, plan, strategize, organize, and mobilize." While reflecting on his words, take into consideration that we are destroying our own communities and deferring our own dreams when we throw bricks and break glass. In the morning the damage is still evident and scattered on the streets in our own neighborhoods.

As disturbing as the issues in our homes and neighborhoods may be, community assembly is a necessity we must not take for granted. If we want the Black children living in these neighborhoods flourishing and growing socially, intellectually, academically, and spiritually, we all must become a positive resource and influence for these youths.

CHAPTER 2:
Education for Life

Whoever said that education is resurrected from a book, encased in one's mind in an isolated cell, or wrapped in the lucid words of a school teacher? Education is not contained solely within the physical structure of an academic institution. The epitome of a true education is really the lessons we learn while traveling down the road of life. Everything we learn along the way, regarding our own individual experiences, becomes a significant part of our life-long learning process. This includes: our relationship with friends and family members, the people we encounter in society, the jobs and careers we venture into, places we visit, the different cultures we explore, and our academic careers spanning from grade school to higher education.

The phrase "Education for Life" encapsulates the learning ideals we internalize as human beings living in a global society. It does not matter which socioeconomic class you are born into because the lessons learned down the road of life are attributed to our unique individual experiences. Reflecting on my own personal life journey, I remember my childhood so vividly, especially the relationships I had with childhood friends, close cousins, aunts and uncles, and my parents and siblings. Although my childhood is not a replica of a Norman Rockwell painting, it is a testimony to my unique and real-life experiences. As a young Black female growing up in Baltimore, my childhood taught me two valuable lessons in life which are, what to do, and what not to do. As an eight year old, I understood the significance of family. I knew that embracing my relationship with my immediate family and close friends who help to sculpture my identity. Each celebration over the holidays and birthdays taught me about unity and togetherness. I studied how we all interacted together, how much we loved, appreciated and supported one another, and the necessity of having a strong family unit.

In society, the initial and most impactful lessons we learn in life take place within our immediate circles. As children, we grow from the knowledge instilled in us from our parents, relatives, and close friends. These relationships are powerful because those interactions cater to one's emotional health and well-being. Human ties govern how we receive the world and how we are perceived by others. Family fosters love and security while friendships enrich our community base. These relationships are strengthened through rich and quality conversations built on trust and an unwavering sense of respect. This is known as the trice leading to a growth turning point in one's life, or the juncture in time when we learn the urgency of human survival and what that process entails.

In my younger years, during times of distress and uncertainty, I would rely on friends and family for guidance and direction. While conferring with my parents, aunts and uncles, I learned about preparation, planning, developing, and refueling my goals. My family taught me that, if you want to secure your future, preparation is an essential aspect of the equation. It is the cornerstone of success which emerges from academic thought. These transitions into the planning process require forethought and a lot of groundwork. The goal is to become educated enough to sustain financially in the world. Either we plan to survive or we plan to fail. That being the case, sometimes we must rearrange, organize, and redesign our life trajectory. To some extent, every man, woman, and child has some control over his or her own future. Developing a comprehensive and constructive plan of action is a recipe for life-long success. These are the tools Black boys and girls need to refuel and meet their academic goals in life.

Life Lessons

In reference to life lessons, during my early twenties, I realized that having good credit, owning a house, buying a car, traveling the world, banking, and understanding the basics in life is about being educated beyond the school building. As a student attending Garrison Junior High School in Baltimore being taught how to calculate numbers, how to type, draw, interpret maps, and how to read and write taught me the basics in academia. However, no one taught me about having a good credit score, no one placed emphasis on higher education, and no one within the confines of any school building I attended asked, what do you want to do when you grow up? This is a common question I often ask my own students just to get them in the mindset of considering their personal and professional options before they reach twelfth grade.

In retrospect, when I think about the other kids from my neighborhood, I realize that the question of future goals may not have been presented to many of them as well. Oftentimes I questioned as a youth, is it a racist expectation that Black boys and girls living in America will not succeed? Is this an outcome that is already preordained, or do we have the ability to change our outcome as individuals? Again, in the words of James Baldwin, it is about rejecting the negative narrative from other ethnic and racial groups. Anyone can attain prestigious heights in their social, personal, and professional lives. It depends on our willpower, commitment, determination, and the education we receive inside and outside of school as we continue down the road of life. I now know that it is both the education I received in the world in addition to the education I received in school that propelled me forward to my current educational, professional and financial status. If I did not learn how to survive in the world, my life could have taken a turn for the worse. But, I managed to stay on the right path and trudge through the storms and roadblocks I encountered along my journey.

In addition to what we are taught in the world, we need to be educated on the reality of having a firm, meaningful, and purposeful instructional education. Students attending public, charter, and private academic institutions need to realize that school is not their personal playground. School is a business and students get paid in grades. No student will receive grades for poor behavior and poor academic performance. Paramount to obtaining true success in life is having the ability and fortitude to look, listen, and learn. Learning is one of the most fundamental processes in life we all experience from birth leading to our death. It is essential that Black mothers and fathers and Black community members in general place emphasis on all aspects of education, so that the children growing up in the inner city or urban areas especially understand and realize that they have a choice, and they have options.

The Education System

Within the educational system in American society, there exists a hierarchy that continues to separate Black students from white students. White students continue to have preferential treatment to private and charter schools while the majority of Black students are confined to urban schools lacking the financial resources necessary for them to compete with their national counterparts. Here, separate but equal is still an ongoing issue for Black Americans. This is the impetus of "racial inequality." For over a century, traveling down the road of equality has been an extremely long and harsh journey for Black students attending public education institutions. Regardless of their knowledge pertaining to these discrepancies and inequalities, school systems across America have not found a permanent and effective remedy to this issue. In reality, like everything else, the needs of the Black student are sacrificed while white students continue to see academic gains in areas such as math, science, and English.

For far too long, American politicians have been ignoring this matter by allocating funding away from the public school system and dismissing the overarching problems that breed in urban education. When it comes to grade school, we as a society must discuss the issues which are housed within these institutions. During the 2018-19 school year, 5.8 percent of the nation's 3.8 million teachers were physically attacked by a student. Almost 10 percent of the teachers during that year were threatened with injury, according to federal education data (Wang, Zhang & Oudekerk, 2020). This statistical information addresses the problem regarding student violence within the urban school system which is another issue preventing Black students from obtaining educational equity. If students are abusing teachers and causing conflict within the learning environment, they are not concentrating on the education process. Instead, the students are becoming the barrier to their own education.

Therefore, the question becomes, what can we do as a race to shift this current state of reality in the urban school system? Should we start arresting students for physical assault on their teachers, or should we find a means to an end to help these students change their negative and dangerous behaviors, so they can lead a meaningful and purposeful existence? These are a few ideas we have to consider if we hope to redirect these students and set them back on the right path in life. However, before anything can be done to cure this problem, teachers, students, parents, and school administrators must reach a consensus on what types of student behaviors are acceptable and what behaviors are not acceptable within the learning environment. This requires the school system to institute a set of universal principles of virtue that can be utilized in schools such as the following:

1. Having students demonstrate a sincerity for being *considerate* about the members of the learning environment including all students and staff.

2. Teach students how to be *courageous* in their pursuit to learn to the best of their ability and to become active and contributing members of the learning environment.

3. Ensure that students understand that they should demonstrate a sense of *confidence* when approaching learning tasks and building positive community relationships.

4. Show students the relevance for demonstrating *caring* behaviors when working alongside teachers and peers.

5. Model the process for approaching learning in a *creative* and productive way, so students can see the benefit in these actions.

Once we are able to teach students how to ascertain these principles and virtues, they can become more efficient and effective learners. More importantly, students will be able to shift away from the negative behaviors and actions which restrict them from excelling academically and begin to gain an appreciation for the set of moral expectations the school system imposes as normative learning behaviors from students in grades k through 12.

Defending Our Right to Learn

Besides the inappropriate and ineffective negative student behaviors resulting in student failure in public schools, racial inequality is another issue which transpires within the very foundation of our urban school buildings. Taking a stance on this matter in question requires an insightful and objective view of the past. Defending our civil and God given rights is a common practice for Black Americans. In the Supreme Court case of *Plessy versus Ferguson,* Homer Plessy demanded that his rights be respected when subjected to being forced to sit in the segregated area of a box car on a train. This is a case of "separate but equal" in which the antagonist in this scenario, Judge John Howard Ferguson, convicted Plessy and charged him with a $25 fine. Later, that conviction is overturned by Justice John Marshall who disagreed with Ferguson's ruling stating that, "separating blacks and whites in public facilities created inequality and marked one race as inferior to another." Regardless of that historical ruling opposing "separate but equal," Blacks are still being subjected to unethical and illegal acts of inequality which separates blacks from whites, especially regarding fairness in education.

It is surreal to ponder on the fact that even though it was established by the Supreme Court in 1896 that the separate facilities were not equal, we continue to live in a world in which the Black men and women are still being treated unfairly as Americans. If the Thirteenth Amendment banned slavery, why are people of color, meaning Black people, not afforded equal protection under the law for any given situation which violates our civil and God given rights as human beings? As an educator for over twenty-five years, I can attest that modern day public school education facilities between blacks and whites are not equal in structure or student outcomes. For instance, white students continue to advance far ahead of their black counterparts by a 20 percent margin on the academic path to success, whereas Black students continue to average way below the academic scale. As it applies to the physical structure of public schools, there are still many buildings which need to be either demolished or rebuilt.

Unfortunately, for over 100 years, facilities and services for people of color compared to whites have not been based on equality, but inequality. Today it is evident that 21st century education is no different from 18th century education as it applies to inequality between the races. White students attending school during the 18th century were sent to preparatory and boarding schools with effective teachers, structured classrooms, and a wealth of materials and technological resources relative to that time period. On the other hand, Blacks were not afforded the right to be educated as a means of protecting the institution of slavery. Sadly enough, current day education conditions for Blacks have not changed all that much when Black children are forced to attend schools without air conditioning during the hot summer months, and subjected to remain in freezing cold buildings during the frigid winter months. All too often this is a trend which resurfaces in highly populated Black schools located in urban areas. Even today, the American government continues to allocate less funding to public school institutions, while funneling more public school funding into white public and charter schools. With this in mind, we come to realize the urgency in our pursuit for establishing education equity in our public schools.

Historically, the hallmark of education in American society, the *Brown vs Board of Education* case was assumed to become the civil rights passage towards educational prosperity for future generations of Black students. This landmark case is established on the premise that laws supporting or establishing racial segregation in public schools are unconstitutional, even if the segregated schools are otherwise equal in quality, noting that quality and equality are not one in the same. In order for black and white education institutions to have a balance in equivalency, the facilities themselves and those things housed within each institution must be equal and identical in both quality and quantity. Today in the year 2020 that remains an illusion. However, as Black Americans, we understand that it is through education that we can fight and neutralize segregation and discrimination forever.

Education Equity

During the Civil Rights Movement, social advocate leaders such as the late Reverend Dr. Martin Luther King Jr., Nelson Mandela, and Malcolm X paved the way for Blacks and other marginalized groups on the road to obtaining educational, financial, social, and economic equality. Each leader addressed issues regarding economics, education, and racial inequality in their speeches to the public as Civil Rights Advocates. In his 1968 speech Dr. King stated, "And as we walk, we must make the pledge that we will always march ahead. We cannot turn back." These words implore us as a race to keep forging ahead to attain our rights and our successes as American citizens. Well aware of the problems that plagued our society like an infected sore, Dr. King worked tirelessly to ensure systemic change in an unjust society. That is when he reminds us later in that same speech that, "We can never be satisfied as long as the negro is the victim of the unspeakable horrors of police brutality" which is something else we as a people must be fully educated on in order to change the dynamics of that reality. If there are two things our black leaders have instilled within us, it is the expectation to be respected as a race, and the knowledge to develop ourselves through education and professional advancement. Taking on their charge we realize that teaching Black students how to become activists for their own learning is an essential aspect of educational equity.

In reference to the teachings from our Black forefathers, Reverend Dr. King, Malcolm X, Nelson Mandela and many other revolutionaries, establishing educational equity is a task that Black Americans must embrace wholeheartedly. Currently, the public education system is not meeting the demands and needs of its Black student population. The lack of funding in public education is a contributing factor to the decline in student success outcomes in academic areas such as math, reading and science. This is because public schools are exclusively funded by the state and local government who in turn reallocate those funds to private and charter schools. In this case one would ponder, how can Black students benefit from an investment which does not exist? The answer is simple, they cannot.

Ironically, the new slogan or paradigm shift in public education is "Equity Education." The ideology behind this phrase is to provide every student in public education with equal learning opportunities. However, in order to execute such a challenging model for economic and educational advancement for all students, a series of variables must be identified and evaluated to determine the probability leading to student success outcomes including:

1. Student participation
2. Family size and structure
3. Student aspirations for learning
4. Parental support in the home
5. School structure and characteristics

In regards to the education system, Black families need to become more involved in the decision making process in reference to the curriculum, school choice, the hiring process, class sizes, school funding, and external programs being integrated in the learning paradigm. The phrase "Education Equity" refers to providing academic excellence and equity for all students. This includes recruiting highly quality teachers and staff, creating functional learning environments free of conflict and distractions for students, and promoting more family and community involvement. However, this seems less of a reality for Black students because the premise caters more to, "The white man's privilege" which does not apply to blacks" (Baldwin, 1984, p. 20). But, by teaching Black boys and girls the value of an education, and helping them strive for academic excellence and achievement we can raise that metaphoric expectation learning bar. We can also decrease the poverty levels for Black Americans within our communities.

To attain this goal, we must ask ourselves, are we trying to keep with common place traditions for Blacks, or are we actually trying to evolve as a people? Keeping with pointless and weightless traditions have not benefited us at all. Our race continues to lag behind other groups in academia, financial wealth, and career attainment. It is time for the Black race to break away from antiquated traditions imposed upon us, and engage in more productive traditions for ourselves and for our children.

This is the ultimate goal for Black America. "For a tradition expresses, after all, nothing more than the long and painful experience of a people; it comes out of the battle waged to maintain their integrity or, to put it more simply, out of their struggle to survive" (Baldwin, 1984, pp. 27-28). This is why education equity is so important to the Black race. Our current generation of youths needs to become well-versed in academics. If not, it will be difficult for them to compete for jobs and careers in this technological and global economy if they are not intellectually apt.

In order to obtain true education equity, we as a people must equip ourselves with 21st century learning paradigms which are reflective of higher education expectations and professional career goals. As we attempt to restore and promote education excellence for our children, we have to engage in the learning process with them in order to guide them effectively through their educational careers. Never should we turn our backs on their academic journey. The moment we turn away, our children can wander off the right path, or venture down the wrong road. To succeed academically, Black students have to be challenged, taught, and guided through the learning process in order for them to gain new knowledge and understand the complexities of the world in which they live. Each of the functioning parts of the education system is unique and compounded. Therefore, in order to assist the Black child, families need to connect more with teachers, administrators, and community organizations. This will help Black families to familiarize themselves with the programs and services available in their communities, so they can effectively help their child reach academic advancement.

Primary Education

Traditionally, the process of learning starts at home, but eventually it branches out into the philosophical classroom. Learning for our youth begins at age 5 in primary education and ends at age 11. Between that timeframe we need to be concerned with how much our students are really learning and what are they not being taught. Sadly enough, the importance of grade school has always been underestimated by most parents in urban

America. They often view primary education as, "The Cute and Cuddly Years." During this education stage, some parents and teachers assume that these five through eleven year old students are too young to have serious and in depth conversations regarding their future goals in life. "They shouldn't have to worry about life," some parents would say. Others would dismiss these precious years as "The Wonder Years." However, we need to stop wondering and start thinking outside the box. How can we ensure that our Black boys and girls are receiving a free, appropriate, and equitable public education? That is the question we must ponder as Black Americans. In recent years, early childhood has come to be seen as a period in which advances in emotion and behavioral regulation and cognitive development prepare children for meeting the social and academic challenges of primary school (Blair & Diamond, 2008). This is a reality which demands our attention and cultivation as parents.

Supposedly, public schools are working towards education equity for all students attending urban institutions. At the primary levels, students are being taught how to read, write, calculate, think critically, and articulate their ideas intellectually as scholars. Basically, for Black students in grades k through 6 attending urban education institutions, these are the pivotal years in their academic careers. This is the time to put away childish ideals and prepare for the future. Starting in kindergarten, students are expected to retell story events and use text evidence to support their ideas. First and second graders are expected to begin reading grade level chapter books and develop paragraphs consisting of a main idea and three or more supporting details. Students in third and fourth grade are conducting scientific investigations using the scientific method and STEM, while fifth and sixth grade students are composing argument papers consisting of 4 or 5 well-developed paragraphs. Basically, students ages five through eleven are expected to participate in an educational platform which is more advanced compared to the days their parents attended grade school. This is how the school systems across America are trying to provide equity education opportunities to minority students, especially those students attending public school institutions.

Secondary Education

When we think about secondary education, we often remember our personal experience in junior high or middle school as young teenagers. We also reminisce about our days in high school as young men and women. Nostalgia as most people call it as we reflect vividly on our childhood past. If we are currently living an ideal life we may embrace that time with admiration and appreciation. On the other hand, if our lives have fallen short of our childhood dreams and expectations, we may look upon that time in our lives with deep regret. It is through the course of our own lives that we consider how valuable, precious, and delicate secondary education is as it applies to the educational experiences of our own children. Keeping that in mind, we understand that once our students' transition into middle school; they often demonstrate difficulty adjusting to both the academic content and the learning environment because this is the time in the student's academic career where he or she is confronted with those roadblocks mentioned in chapter one of this book.

For most teenagers, middle school is a time of discovery. In the content of English Language Arts, especially in Literature, we call it, "Coming of Age." This is the point in the teenager's life where he or she discovers who he or she is as an intellectual as well as a human being. In that sense, students in grades 6 through 12 are comparable to flowers. They bloom at different rates, grow in different directions, demonstrate multiple personalities, have different experiences, and demonstrate different levels of stability. At this level of their academic careers, many students manage to survive the middle school experience. Some matriculate successfully into high school while others fail drastically, due to peer pressure and outside influences. Unfortunately, those students who do not come into themselves and claim their individual identities become lost and self-destructive. They often end up repeating grades, creating conflict in the classroom, or they just reject the education system altogether and end up dropping out of school.

Regardless if a student manages to matriculate from middle school to high school, he or she will continue to need parental support and academic guidance. Learning is an extensive, in-depth, and ongoing intellectual process. Parents cannot afford to "drop the ball" just because their student has transitioned into the high school environment. For the most part, relying on a broken education system is unproductive and ineffectual. It is time to be more assertive in our academic pursuits for our children. Young Black boys and girls deserve a better future than their parents. They should truly be given the opportunity to obtain intellectual knowledge which can lead to a profitable and productive career. Preparing middle and high school students to obtain equity in education will demand student dedication, diligence, and practice. It also demands equitable funding from the state and local government, and there has to be a greater investment in public education across America.

Creating Education Equity for Black Students

As a Black father raising two sons, ensuring that my children are receiving an equitable education is one of my main priorities in life. My job is to make sure my kids first realize the importance of their education, not just by telling but by giving clear examples of the results of a person's efforts when it comes to their education. For example, I don't shy away from taking my kids to my old neighborhood and let them speak with the adults that sold drugs and hung out on the street corners as kids and never saw value in educating themselves as they became adults. Another example would be taking my children to see a college basketball game with a future NBA prospect and then follow him to his dorm room afterwards as he prepares his evening for study. I would ask him to talk to my sons about his goals and the things he has to sacrifice to achieve them. Now these examples do not solve the problem we face with keeping our kids with active minds focused on education and the task of being successful, but it does lean towards providing effective strategies to have kids respect the opportunities that education provides.

From a parental perspective, I understand that to ensure that my sons attain equity in education I have to be an active participant in their academic careers. Furthermore, I need to ensure that teachers are helping my sons solidify what they are learning in school. How do I do this? One way of doing this is by volunteering at the school. As a Black male, I choose to be a role model or a mentor as some would call it. Spending time at your child's school allows you to get a true view of the culture of the school. Teachers will not be able to hide who they truly are as you get familiar with the climate of the school. When teachers see parents prioritizing their child's educational needs and providing support within the school building, they are more encouraged to place emphasis on student learning outcomes. In my opinion, parent involvement also encourages students to engage more in the learning process, and can also build a child's self-esteem. Students who see their parents investing in their education start to invest more themselves.

With regards to education equity and ensuring productivity is taking place in the learning environment; educators need to ensure that Black boys and girls are receiving a quality education. This means teachers in grades k through 12 are approaching the 21st century teaching paradigm with the intent on effectively measuring student achievement in all content areas, demonstrating a sense of fairness towards all students, and providing students with repeated opportunities to advance themselves within the educational arena, while keeping in mind that not all students interpret information the same, and not all students approach learning in the same manner. The two main factors here are fairness and inclusion. As a father, and more importantly as a Black man raising two sons, I intend on ensuring that my sons are being treated fairly as scholars and being fully included in the education process. Historically, education has always shaped us as individuals. It separates the "Haves" from the "Have Nots," and the "Successful" from the "Unsuccessful." That is why I am dedicated to ensuring that my sons have access to programs and strategies both within and outside of school that will empower and equip them as young men to succeed both academically and professionally.

Remain Steadfast in the Pursuit for Education

Keep in mind that pursuing a quality and equitable education is not your basic marathon. Instead, it is a race for equality in education and future productivity outcomes for Black boys and girls especially. This is truly a life changing event because it is the most important denominator for their future success. Within the public school system, the teacher is the one in the driver's seat and the students are the passengers. They are the precious cargo we are responsible for getting from one level in education to the next. According to Gregory and Kuzmich (2004), "Teaching is sometimes like riding a bobsled; we need to stay in a certain groove on the icy course to maximize the speed and smoothness of a run" (p. 30). If we as educators expect for students to excel academically, we must be in our driver seat ready to steer the course of learning. In addition to teacher responsibilities, as Black families and members of the Black community, we must never waver in our pursuit for equality. We must remain steadfast in our purpose. We must commit to the promise of helping our Black youth excel academically and socially in an effort to ensure that they are able to fulfill their dreams, and become productive and competent members of society.

The idea that it is too late to change the course of our history is a farce and another false narrative which I personally reject as a Black woman, educator, and mother of three. As long as there is breath in our bodies and the human spirit contained within our souls, we should always remain hopeful. Since learning is a long and extensive process, we will always have enough time to make a difference in the lives of our youth. Teaching students how to self-regulate and become independent thinkers, reflective facilitators of their own learning, and great decision makers in the learning community helps them to reach academic competency in all aspects of their educational career in grades k through 12. Parents, teachers, administrators, and community members should never place limits on student success because all students are capable of learning.

However, two questions remain: are we willing to build up our communities, or are we willing to watch them fall? In that respect, as community members, we must be truly conscientious about what is really happening within our communities in order to stop the oppression, and remember that each one must teach one. There is a constant reminder in urban America that Black boys and girls continue to lag way behind their white counterparts on the academic threshold of education. Therefore, parents cannot place the complete confidence of their child's education in the hands of the school system. It takes a village to raise a child. The village in this scenario consists of parents, teachers, neighbors, grandparents, friends, and the community at large.

Educating the Black Student

The first step to understanding how to properly educate the Black student is to understand the history of America. Not the white history, but the Black experience. Just like a black man can never be white, the white man can never know what it is like to be born Black in America. White education has always and continues to be based on privilege whereas Black education is based on centuries of oppression, brutality, and the human struggle. During the 1950s racial segregation in public schools was the norm. America embraced the separation of Black and white students in public learning institutions causing decades of division between the races. For instance, whenever Black students tried to attend segregated schools in the Confederate South and in several northern states, they were confronted with racial opposition. These students were beaten, dragged, abused, spit on, shamed, sprayed with water by high power hoses, and placed in jail for standing up for their rights as American born citizens.

Their only crime is that they wanted to obtain the American Dream by way of education. In *Brown versus Board of Education in Topeka (1954),* the Supreme Court unanimously declared racial segregation in public schools as unconstitutional because it violated the fourteenth amendment to the United States Constitution. Even though the law was imposed by the supreme court, many school districts continued to demonstrate their animosity and blatant refusal to comply with the court's decision. In retrospect, it was the institution of the National Association for the Advancement of Colored People

(NAACP) in 1909 that a movement against inequality in America began to actively emerge. The goal of the NAACP was to eliminate racial discrimination and segregation from American society. This was in itself an admirable plight. In spite of all their efforts, today we continue to seek advancement for people of color, especially the advancement of Black boys and girls living in urban communities.

Another thing to understand regarding the Black experience in America is police brutality. What Black boys and girls witness on the news and view on social media regarding the number of Black men and women who were senselessly murdered by police and racist white Americans have a bearing on their worldview? These students begin to question their own mortality when they see Black teenagers being murdered for walking down the street, or being Black while sleeping in their own homes. This does something to the human psyche. On several occasions during my career, I remember students asking me, Dr. Washington, what did you think about Trayvon Martin getting shot by George Zimmerman. Or, why did that cop have to kill George Floyd? Instead of teaching language arts and literature to my students, I had to discuss race relations and the social injustices Blacks are subjected to in America.

Needless to say, the issue of race continues to be an overarching problem in American society. Even in the public school building race issues have a way of emerging in the classroom and alter the trajectory of the education process for the young Black student. How can our students receive a free, appropriate, and public education based on equity outcomes if the true essence of equality and fairness does not exist? Enough is enough! When will the Black youth receive the quality education he or she deserves based on a learning environment which is free of distractions which impede his or her social, emotional, and academic growth? Until something is done to alleviate and lessen racial tensions in America, Black youth will always be subjected to racial bias.

The Ultimate Education Lesson

Besides the lessons taught at home and within the public school system, the Black experience will always be the true lessons Black boys and girls need to be taught. The Black youth need to be aware of the fact that systemic racism is a major issue in American society and that as a race we need to advocate for our rights as American citizens. Within the year 2020 alone, as a race, we have lost too many of our Black men and women to acts of racial violence at the hands of racist police officers and racist white supremacists who devalue our status as Americans. Teaching our Black boys and girls about the Black experience is an essential aspect of their education. It is an unfortunate and disturbing reality they need to be aware of as American citizens living in a society consumed with racist hate. We should never underestimate the impact of racism involving educational outcomes for our Black students because race continues to be a major factor regarding the productivity performances of students of color who attend urban schools in America.

As a given, the major teaching principle is to know your students. This is done by learning about the Black culture and their experiences as a group of marginalized people. How can Black children be properly educated when they do not have a voice, or are not being recognized as a race group in the books being utilized in public schools for instructional purposes? The majority of the books Black students read in school are based on white lead characters from the white perspective. These racist narratives are only used to cater to "the white man's privilege" by excluding the Black male and female lead characters from these book roles. A lack or absence of Black character led books is a form of systemic racism because it uses literature to criticize or vanquish a race of people from the narrative. Black children need to see a reflection of themselves in the books they read in school. This is how we uplift Black boys and girls intellectually and spiritually, so they can see their value in the world. Unfortunately, within the walls of the educational institution there is no escaping race, especially when inequality continues to be a catastrophic windfall in our country.

Race relations in the United States of America are at their highest peak. Even with the COVID-19 outbreak, racial violence against Black Americans and other forms of social injustice continues to emerge in this country. These acts of racial hatred continue to reveal its gruesome face and spin its ugly head. Despite the pandemic our country is currently experiencing, and the high death rate surge in our communities, systemic racism within society is surpassing the disease itself. With that being said, it appears that a diseased mind consumed with racial epithets is more important than a human life. But, sadly those ideals do take precedence in the eyes of the racist.

For the most part, the ultimate education lesson revolves around our ability as Black Americans to change the trajectory of our past by creating a more productive future for Black boys and girls in this country. We do this by speaking and acting on their behalf as our forefathers Reverend Dr. Martin Luther King, Malcolm X, and Nelson Mandela in addition to many other Black Civil Rights Advocates did for us many years ago. If not, this insurmountable issue called systemic racism will continue to demolish our race and keep us in a confined mental, emotional, and physical prison.

CHAPTER 3:
Intellectual Advancement and Achievement

Although intellectual advancement and achievement leads to professional and financial success, many Americans, especially Black Americans, have yet to obtain that level of triumph collectively as a group. While America is the richest country in the world, it is also the most unequal. Currently, there are forty million people living in poverty which is approximately 12 percent of the American population. This is mostly due to inequality issues which emerge in the United States. Of that number, 21.2 percent of Blacks are living well-below the poverty line compared to whites who fall only 8.7 percent below the poverty scale. Even by today's standards, this remains a common trend in our country.

Additionally, even though poverty in America has decreased over the past three years, income inequality in our country has increased significantly. There are approximately more employed White Americans compared to high levels of unemployed Black Americans which is a troubling statistic. The population ratio of white to black Americans living in this country is 76.3 percent to 13.4 percent the remainder being other races of people. With 78 percent of the workforce being white, this is why it is imperative that Black Americans continue to achieve intellectual advancement, so that their families can reap the benefits of socioeconomic achievement and growth. With that in mind, many scenarios may emerge in the form of a series of questions such as, what does it mean to be intellectually competent? Who in society determines competency? How is this process initiated, and what is the significance of obtaining intellectual advancement and achievement? This leads me to reflect on the first question regarding intellectual competency.

Intellectual Competency

As it relates to the learning process, there is no "cookie-cutter" answer or solution to obtaining intellectual competency. One size does not fit all. As human beings we learn differently and we approach world education from multiple perspectives. Our intellectual preferences are as unique as our clothing style. For instance, if one does not care about his or her appearance regarding presentation of self, I doubt if he or she is going to be concerned about intellectual affairs. Regardless, be that as it may, we all need to obtain some level of intellectual growth and competency.

The context is that people demonstrate a variation of eight unique learning styles which include: (1) logical/mathematical, (2) Linguistic, (3) Musical, (4) Spatial, (5) Bodily-Kinesthetic, (6) Naturalistic, (7) Interpersonal, and (8) Intra-personal (Gardner, 1998). While reflecting on our individual learning styles we must analyze and evaluate how we are allowing ourselves to access, process, and internalize the information we receive from others. This information can originate from various sources such as the community in which we live, our local schools, political leaders, people we associate with, and most importantly derive from our own families. Therefore, the concept of education can never be isolated to the confines of a school building. Anyone we encounter in our lives impacts what we learn in addition to altering our belief system as we grow intellectually.

In explaining the meaning of intellectual competence, I would describe it as one's ability to demonstrate how something is done, or how things work in the world. To reach this type of competency, one does not have to be the most astute person in American society, but I would hope that he or she would aspire to becoming a well-educated and intelligent human being. Ignoring one's self-worth and one's capability as an intellectual is a hindrance which prevents one from moving productively forward in life. All too often in the Black race, this is a roadblock we often are confronted with when it comes to personal advancement and achievement in the public school system, in the workplace, and within our own communities.

Intellectually competent human beings are proficient and comprehensive learners who have an overabundance of wisdom. These scholarly individuals are keen on advancing themselves in school and in the workplace. They take pride in their accomplishments and demonstrate an impressive work ethic. Moreover, they see their hard work as being based on principle and worthy of reward. That is why they put so much time and effort into what they do. These individuals try their best to perfect their skills and talents making them the best of the best in both the academic and professional arena.

As a race, we do need to put forth more effort when it comes to educating our Black boys and girls. Too often our students are being promoted from one grade to the next without the intellectual ability to sustain themselves in the real-world. For intellectual competency to be a reality for the Black student, parents, teachers, administrators, and other stakeholders have to be committed to helping them excel as scholars. One can not become competent enough to survive in this world if he or she is not provided with the academic tools to gain employment, or the knowledge to transition into higher education and beyond.

Therefore, the road to intellectual competence for students starts with students assuming responsibility for their own learning, the teacher's ability to educate the student effectively based on his or her knowledge of curriculum and pedagogy, and his or her ability to address the academic needs of each student in the classroom. On the other end of that spectrum are the parents. Learning must initially take place at home. Parents need to become active members of the student learning process meaning they should be inquiring about homework, class assignments, and testing while assisting their children academically when needed. Parents also need to build positive and productive relationships with teachers, and attend teacher-parent conferences to keep themselves abreast of their child's academic progress.

How Is Competency Determined

Whether we are scholars of academics or world scholars, we obtain knowledge through effective, meaningful, and purposeful teachings. But, those instructional practices must cater directly to the need of each individual student, not just to the class as a whole. Regardless if you are a parent or a teacher, it is a known fact that all students learn at different rates and view learning from multiple perspectives. Yet, school systems continue to assume that students learn alike and think the same. In classrooms across America, students are being taught the same "cookie-cutter" curriculum, and expected to learn at the same pace. This is a dangerous misconception that continues to frustrate the Black student, and obstruct his or her path towards intellectual competency, especially because this teaching practice is both unproductive and ineffectual.

Until we as a society realize that the "cookie-cutter" teaching approach does not work, nor address the educational needs of the Black student, we will continue to see our students struggling as scholars and falling way below the academic curve. The education system has to adjust the curriculum to fit the student, not try to fit the student to the curriculum. Students, who do not feel comfortable in the learning community because of their learning deficits and marginalized learning competencies get easily bored, lose interest in the learning process, or they become major behavior problems in the classroom. Student competency levels are determined by their aggressive and assertive approach towards learning, their ability to analyze, evaluate, and interpret what is being taught, and their ability to conceptualize the learning process as independent and critical thinkers.

The Competency Process

There are a series of processes and steps taken in order to achieve one's academic goals. This undertaking is extremely demanding and requires active academic exercise on behalf of the learner. There is an internal drive within all of us that we must connect with to bring forth our desire and aspiration to surpass any external limitation the world places at our feet. This emerging drive is housed deep within ourselves and is often identified as free-will, self-motivation, or an internal drive. Since the beginning of our existence, we have been questioning our purpose in life and wondering what road to travel to reach academic, professional and financial success. The process is clear. It all starts with self-internalization which encompasses the guiding principles through which learning and socialization are born. If you want something done, you have to be willing to put in the time, the effort, and the work needed to reach your goals. If life was easy, everyone would be successful. We would not even be having this conversation about acquiring intellectual advancement and achievement. Instead, we would be sitting on a beach in Maui sipping tropical cocktails.

But, the reality is that the negative stereotypes, brutal assaults and killings inflicted on the Black race over the course of history, in addition to social injustices instituted by racist politicians, and the dysfunctional home environment have all had a bearing on the current state of inequality for Blacks in America. However, we cannot waste another second worrying about "The White Man," or continue feeling sorry for ourselves. As a race of people, we need to focus our concern and energy on our Black boys and girls, so we can determine what can be done to change the dynamics of their current academic nightmares. Someone once asked me, how did you make it when those around you gave up? My response was clear. I replied by saying, "I dug deep within myself, I prayed to God for guidance and direction, and I never gave up." To this day, I attribute my intellectual competence and professional success to my spiritual beliefs and my internal drive to persevere in this world. In my opinion, people become who they believe they are in this life. For instance, if you believe you can excel in school, and have the ability to attend a university and become a career professional, it will happen based on that sheer will. On the opposite side of that spectrum, if you do not view yourself as a competent, valued, capable, and deserving human being, you may end up creating your own barriers in life, and possibly attributing to your own demise.

The Three Levels of Academic Competency

There are three overarching elements which lead to academic competency. They are the skills, attitudes, and behaviors of the student which leads to his or her academic success. Within the learning community be it school, home, or the public, students are learning rapidly about the world in which they live. Those teachings can be either effective, or they can be ineffective. As parents and educators we have to monitor those teachings with a keen eye. This means that as the instructors to our Black boys and girls, we have to become the overseer to their educational journey. Think about this task as being "A Call to Action" because it is our actions which will dictate their future successes or failures.

Besides the student, the parents and teachers are responsible for motivating, directing, supporting, and modeling the concepts of learning. After all, learning is an in-depth and critical process which can be time consuming and calculating if not embraced fully with the intent of achieving one's academic and professional goals. Gregory and Kuzmich (2004) stated how, "Being cognizant of learning styles and preferences is another lens through which we know our learners and respond to their interests and needs" (p. 7). These ideals are still relevant today as we come to a resolution on how to cater to the individual learning needs of the Black student.

In regards to the skills, attitudes, and behaviors that students demonstrate within the learning environment, we understand that each of these elements require dedication on behalf of students, parents, and teachers. Furthermore, we know that it takes a village to raise a child. Therefore, it will take a lot for a student to reach academic competency. Knowing that positive learning experiences influence and encourage positive learning outcomes students need a consistent dose of parental and teacher sponsorship in gearing them towards the right path in life. This is based on several learning systems that are represented in our daily lives which include catering to a child's emotional, social, cognitive, and reflective needs.

All students need emotional support because they constantly question themselves and often demonstrate self-doubt which causes them to experience moments of low self-esteem. During the social learning process, students interact with peers and demonstrate learning behaviors that are either externally or internally developed, or a combination of both. The reflective aspect of learning involves having the ability to self-internalize through personal reflection. This is when the student reflects on his or her ability as a learner, and questions his or her level of success and failure. Moving forward in our pursuit to establish economic and educational equity for our Black boys and girls, we must focus more on effective instructional methods and techniques that connect with their learning styles, interests, preferences, and addresses their social and emotional as well as their academic needs.

Focusing on the Whole Child

Believe it or not, educating Black boys and girls requires a holistic teaching approach. It demands the full participation of the family and the educator. Just as a student cannot be expected to educate him or herself in the areas of mathematics, science, reading, writing, and history, an educator alone cannot teach the student everything he or she needs to learn in life. Parents and teachers have to work collaboratively to ensure the student succeeds academically at each of the chronological grade levels. This requires everyone involved to educate the whole child. The teacher provides the external motivation at school through daily instruction while the parents reinforce the teacher's actions by providing the emotional and parental support and guidance the student needs at home. This creates a unified infrastructure for the student to depend on when he or she needs assistance during the learning stages in life. The collaborative efforts of the teacher and parents also help the student to build his or her intrinsic motivation skills. In turn, the student becomes more self-sufficient and independent as a learner throughout the course of his or her academic journey.

For far too long, we have stood idly by in a silent stance while students of color have been falling through the cracks in the education system. Young male and female Black students in grades k through 12 have been denied an efficient and quality learning experience to prepare them for future college and careers. Instead of teaching Black boys and girls scientific concepts regarding Biological, Environmental, and Molecular Science on an in depth level, our students have been taught the bare minimum. Black students are often deterred from taking AP courses that focus on major research areas that can benefit them in the future by helping them to become potential scientists and engineers. These are science areas where Black students lag behind their white counterparts. If we want to change the trajectory of their academic knowledge and prepare them for productive careers, we need to expose them to courses that are beneficial to their future success.

As advocates for social justice and supporters of the Black Lives Matter Movement, we need to focus on educating the whole child. Different learning styles demand different measures of instruction for students. During the observation process in the classroom, the teacher is able to ascertain student preferences regarding their unique learning styles, so he or she can cater to their various academic needs. This requires the educator to be extremely observant while monitoring student learning behaviors during the instructional process. Creating a supportive, encouraging, and safe learning environment is a crucial aspect of this instructional exercise. Students need to believe that they are valued and respected by teachers and peers alike. To confirm student beliefs regarding their value in the classroom, the decision making process should be a mutual endeavor between teacher and student. Moreover, the student in collaboration with the teacher should be self-monitoring his or her work and productivity outcomes in the classroom on a biweekly basis.

At present, the learning outcomes for the Black student is a matter of urgency essentially due to the fact that too many of our youth are significantly failing academically in the areas of reading, math, and science, and many are graduating from high school on a fifth grade reading level. Knowing these devastating outcomes, teachers and school administrators must consider how students are learning, and determine what strategies need to be implemented in the instructional paradigm to build upon the academic needs of each individual student. This can be done by having students respond to a series of self-reflection inventory questions regarding their learning preferences. For instance, one could ask, do you like new challenges, or do you prefer solving math and science problems step by step? Another way to evaluate student learning preferences is by using a teacher observation checklist regarding student learning behaviors in each of the aforementioned content categories. This entails monitoring student skill ability levels in the classroom, evaluating their attitudes towards learning, being aware of their social interaction with other students, and recognizing their precision for utilizing previously taught strategies to solve learning problems.

In his book *Push Yourself: No More Excuses,* Kamal M. Sanders (2011) asserts that, "During a certain age, students should begin to take some sort of responsibility because they are preparing for life after high school" (p. 56). This is an obvious and relevant point since one's grade school education is preparation for college and the workforce. Students in this instance become the leaders of learning by taking control of their academic journey. This prompts the student to gain a deeper insight into his or her knowledge as a member of the learning community. At this stage, through use of journaling, the student begins to ask him or herself the following questions, what was difficult for me to understand today? If I could redo this assignment or activity, what would I do differently, or what can I do next time to improve my grade? These are just a few internal concepts which may emerge while students are self-reflecting on the learning process and beginning to take ownership of their own learning.

Formal Education

The concept of education is perceived from multiple perspectives. The different ways we view learning are based on our own interpretations in addition to how we internalize the information we are given. One way education is introduced, interpreted, and explained is from a formal viewpoint. Formal education refers to the primary, secondary, and college teachings a student receives on his or her academic journey in life. Furthermore, formal education is one of America's pathways which lead its citizens to achieving economic productivity and prosperity. Grajcevci and Shala (2016) define the formal aspect of education by stating, "Formal education is an organized education model, structured and administered by laws and norms, and subject to strict curriculum objectives, methodology and content" (p. 119). This involves a precedent of teaching and learning based on structured principles of education from both a political and economical perspective. When teaching the Black student, it is not about micromanaging, it is about catering to the intellectual and diverse needs of the learner.

Formal structures and approaches to teaching are used in the public school setting across the United States of America. The American education system places emphasis on using a curriculum that is uniformed across states. Even though several states follow their own education agenda, the majority of the states in this country use the same curriculum in the areas of mathematics, science, and language arts. By using expert information during the instructional process, and modeling analytical thinking skills and behaviors to students, educators hope to create a learning environment built on academic competency. Providing constant feedback to students and reflecting on their academic standing and performance in the classroom are essential factors related to getting them to take ownership of their learning and to help students become active and competent learners.

In short, formal education is a systematic process in which students enter grade school at the kindergarten level, and transition from one academic level to the next until they graduate from twelfth grade. The kindergarten level is where students learn about self-control, are taught how to build their social skills through an instructional routine called social skill development, learn how to listen carefully while following teacher directives, and learn how to share and cooperate with others. At this stage students are taught how to behave according to social norms and expectations in addition to being taught how to interact with their peers in a social setting. Kindergarten is also the grade where students first begin learning how to read, write, calculate basic arithmetic problems, and engage in the scientific method. By first grade, students begin to build their self-confidence as scholars through continuous practice with academic routines. Second graders are more inquisitive at this academic stage. This grade level of students is more attuned with the intricacies of the educational process. Third graders are at that discovery stage where they need to know the answer to every question and every possible scenario.

However, by the time students reach fourth through fifth grade, a type of evolution begins. Fourth graders are more independent learners who are fully capable of utilizing previously taught skills to help them navigate through the curriculum. Their choice of social preferences usually emerges during this educational stage. Moreover, the curriculum load becomes twice as challenging for learners in fourth grade due to the increase in content rigor and complexity. By fifth grade, students get used to the workload, they are engaged in the learning process and begin to take ownership of their own learning. Students begin to evolve and mature quickly by fifth grade. These students learn how to balance and manage their instructional time effectively, and they are great at organizing and planning. Fifth grade is the final grade in elementary school for these scholars. They have been preparing themselves for years for the transition into middle school. For some fifth graders the academic transition from elementary to secondary school will be easy, for others it will prove to be an enormous challenge and undertaking if they are not intellectually and mentally prepared.

As it relates to secondary school, especially for grades 6 through 8, students need to be academically, socially, mentally, and intellectually prepared as scholars. For the record, middle school can be overwhelmingly difficult for the average youth. This is an extremely demanding stage within one's academic career because students are expected to complete a massive amount of work. At the middle school stage in grade school, students are responsible for their learning and they are expected to approach each learning situation with professionalism and accuracy. They should demonstrate a willingness to do their scholarly jobs, and produce quality work making them worthy to transition into high school by the end of eighth grade. The more effective and appropriate learning behaviors students demonstrate at this academic stage dictates their readiness level for high school. If they can complete their community learning hours, earn good grades in all content areas, or generate a passing grade point average by the end of the eighth grade year, they would have met the learning expectations for matriculation. Then, students are ready for the transition to the next stage in their academic careers.

The final stage in formal education regarding grade school is the high school level. Here students are ready to work towards their future dreams and aspirations by preparing themselves for college and the workforce. Learning at this stage becomes more of a necessity than a burden. High school students understand that they are moving towards adulthood, and that their childhood years are way behind them. For most students, this is a turning tide in their lives. Some students become fearful about the future at this stage while others embrace this opportunity with such hope and appreciation. Although high school is an exciting experience for most students, it can be a devastating experience for Black boys and girls who find they are struggling academically in the majority of their core courses. This is an issue which currently exists in highly Black populated academic institutions, especially those schools located in urban communities. That is why it is essential for urban school districts to incorporate new teaching technologies in education, and implement usage of teaching digital competencies in the instructional curriculum because 21st century education demands a new perspective regarding student engagement and learning practices.

Informal Education

Opposite to the processes of formal education, the concept of an informal education relates to how a student is exposed to lessons learned in the real-world. It does not involve a systematic process. These lessons can be taught in a variety of settings. An informal education is raw in introduction and delivery. Some students find this teaching and learning technique to be extremely student friendly and less formal because it is more interactive and engaging compared to formal strategies of instruction. The activities and tools used during informal instruction provides students with the necessary resources to analyze and evaluate complex learning tasks through more hands-on learning opportunities. These lessons are student centered in the sense that they focus on the student interest pertaining to topics covered in the curriculum. Informal education is a casual process where students are engaged in conversations surrounding the curriculum in which the learning process is more exploratory and discovery based. Moreover, students are more likely to reach multiple levels of success during informal instruction. Regardless of the scenario, having an informal education is another series of learning events students experience on their academic journey in life.

Another concept regarding informal education is that it relates to lessons learned outside of the school building as well. This applies to periods of instruction, mentoring, and tutoring a student receives outside of the school environment. Instead of the educator teaching the student, parents, friends, family, and possibly community members are the instructors during this learning process. A child may meet with a tutor at a local library and practice reading, math, and science skills with the tutor. At home, the parent could teach the child about measurements using the metric system while teaching him or her how to cook and bake. The student can learn about gravity while riding a bike or skateboarding in the neighborhood. Even though informal learning is not an intentional learning process, it is highly effective in most cases because it promotes self-directed learning exercises on the student's behalf. Additionally, it involves social networking, a series of coaching and mentoring opportunities for the student, and it also allows the student to take ownership of the learning. This process provides the student with more exposure to building real-world knowledge of academic concepts.

During this instructional phase, the student is exposed to strategies that increase and improve his or her skill base for future use in life. These are things we learn from childhood to adulthood. This is what we call "life-long" learning skills. As human beings we learn day in and day out, and year after year without limitation. The question is, how do we utilize and retain the information that we learn throughout the course of our lives? I recall as a child, being taught by my mother how to brush my teeth, match my clothes, tie my shoes, and count money. My big brother was the one who taught me how to draw, cook, and how to protect myself in a street fight. My aunts were the ones who taught me about women's things. As far as taking care of a home, my mother taught me how to decorate, pay bills, paint and wallpaper, and the importance of keeping a clean and organized home. Even now, I remember those teachings and appreciate the lessons I have been taught. With that being said, it is easy to understand the fundamentalism behind informal education, especially since this teaching and learning model epitomizes the concept of, "It takes a village to raise a child." After all, the world is our classroom.

Spiritual Education

Having a spiritual foundation is essential to becoming a loving, respectful, caring, and humane individual. This is indeed a valuable lesson all children need to learn in life. Too often, I have witnessed situations in urban school environments where students curse out teachers and other students, act aggressively, and make verbal threats towards teachers and peers. In my mind I wonder, what kind of spiritual foundation do these students have in their lives, or do they attend Sunday school to learn about God? Everyone has a right to believe in and practice their own religion. They also have the right to worship their own God. However, if there is no spiritual foundation, how can we expect for them to understand the basic concepts of respecting and honoring others. When I was a child, I used to attend church on a regular basis. There was always someone in the neighborhood going to church early on Sunday morning. If I didn't catch a ride with Ms. Odessa, I could get a ride with Ms. Hayes. Those two women never missed a day of church. Unlike me, my brothers and sisters would always play outside on Sunday morning, but I answered to a higher calling. I needed to hear the word. I was always attracted to learning the gospel even at a very young age.

Divine is the Lord. I remember those vivid and calming words even today. As a child, hearing those words let me know that there was something greater than myself in this world. Those words gave me hope as a child, and I held on to that hope. You see, children definitely need something to believe in to guide them through life. Without guidance, children get lost. I have witnessed so many of my childhood friends get lost to the streets. They put their faith in man before God. From a parental and educational standpoint, I know that we as a people cannot afford to lose anymore of our Black boys and girls to the world. They need our guidance, support, direction, and protection, but most of all they need the word of God. Unfortunately, sometimes we take our spiritual beliefs for granted not realizing how crucial these spiritual teachings can impact a child's life for the better. When human beings believe in something higher than themselves, they are more geared towards making the right decisions in life.

Therefore, we must remember that on the road in life, one path is a spiritual journey and the other path is not.

Regardless of the path we take in life, the journey is our own. This is a choice we make based on our own personal preferences in life. If one values religion, he or she will live his or her life from a spiritual perspective. On the other hand, if that person values the streets more, he or she sees no value in religion. Spiritual education is something we are exposed to at birth during our baptism if our family has a religious background and ties to the church. However, if that religious foundation is absent from our lives, there is no spiritual belief system to reflect upon. Fortunately, obtaining spiritual guidance and developing a spiritual relationship with God is always an available option for all human beings, but keep in mind that our religious beliefs are not isolated to the church building. Having faith in a higher power is an internal factor which aids in building one's character. Moreover, religion and spirituality are the very fibers of one's moral compass which guides one on the right path in life. Without that spiritual background there is no direction. When we accept the word of God, we reject the word of man, especially the word of men with the intent to destroy or ruin our lives.

Socialization and humanization Within the School Setting

Students must be taught the importance of effective and constructive socialization techniques. This involves modeling positive and effective learning behaviors that are expected norms related to being a productive and earnest citizen. These are basic human behaviors which demonstrate one's ability to be a cordial, empathetic, sincere, friendly, genial, and a good-natured human being. One of the things we know to be true in life is that behavior is taught and learned. Students internalize what they observe and emulate those behaviors. These behaviors can be taught in a formal learning community or adopted from an informal learning environment. In spite of how the learning takes place, the student still replicates those behaviors in his or her actions when interacting with others in a social setting. Basically, the student actions stem directly from the social learning paradigm. "Key to this sense of agency is the fact that, among other personal factors, individuals possess self-beliefs that enable them to exercise a measure of control over their thoughts, feelings, and actions, that "what people think, believe, and feel affects how they behave" (Bandura, 1986, p. 25). In layman's terms, our belief system guides and dictates our actions. We demonstrate what we learn, and from what we observe in life. Then, we emulate and model those behaviors through our own actions.

Holistically, these social behaviors can either make us good citizens or turn us into corrupt individuals. It all depends on the behaviors we observe and internalize during our formal and informal education, but also keeping in mind that without a spiritual foundation individual lose their way in life seeking direction from the outside world. To ensure that students are being humanized and socialized appropriately and properly in the school setting requires a series of academic and observational checks and balances. During this process, we should be inquiring, are students demonstrating appropriate learning behaviors in the classroom setting? Do we hear students using inappropriate language when speaking to staff members and peers, or were students on task, and not disruptive during instruction?" These are just a few minor questions we can focus on when considering whether or not students are demonstrating positive social behavior skills while interacting with teachers and peers. This is important because students need to understand that positive social actions promote expected and effective human behaviors.

Consequently, students who are not well-versed in using positive learning etiquette often demonstrate inappropriate and inhumane behaviors in the learning environment which tend to disrupt the academic setting and postpone learning opportunities for other students. These types of behaviors are both unfortunate and unacceptable in any type of learning environment. Parents, teachers, and community members need to work collaboratively to promote positive learning behaviors for Black youth. With everything happening in the world including the recurring episodes of social injustice, it is time we take a stand and make some real change happen in our urban communities and schools. We are the instructors in their lives. Therefore, we must organize our efforts to find a permanent resolution to various behavior issues our children continue to express through their actions. If we do not help the Black student, they will be lost forever. This is a new year, but nothing has changed. Black boys and girls are still failing at massive rates within the public school system. They desperately need our assistance in getting them where they need to be on their academic journey. Without a quality education based on equity and opportunity, our youth will not be able to compete with their white counterparts in this global economy.

Academic Advancement in a Changing Society

Student strengths, needs, abilities, and their academic preferences all have an impact on the level of achievement they obtain from grade school to college. The way students interpret learning, and the value they place on the learning process determines their success outcome. Students should always be aware of their propensity as learners. The attitudes they express within the formal and informal learning environment indicates their effort as scholars and future workers. Learning demands involvement on behalf of the teaching instructor and the student. Learning is never a one sided, or an isolated process. It consists of a series of factors including: effective instructional delivery, execution of a lesson, student engagement in the learning environment, and a mutual respect between student and teacher.

In order to ascertain whether or not, Black boys and girls are benefiting from their education, teachers need to assess them on a regular basis. Preferably teachers will assess students weekly if not on a biweekly basis depending on the skills he or she is monitoring. If students are not aware of their inconsistencies with learning, and educators are not checking for understanding, student learning issues cannot be resolved. That is why it is important to provide weekly feedback to students, so they can begin to self-monitor their learning behaviors. At some point, students must take responsibility for their actions in the classroom by advocating for their own learning. Everyone has a voice. Therefore, students need to speak up and defend their own rights to obtain an equitable and quality education.

CHAPTER 4:
College Choice

Most Black Americans never get to attend college due to financial constraints or limitations or not having a high school diploma to get them in the door. Sometimes their reasons for not attending college are family related. Maybe their mother or father never went to college, or maybe going to college was never a discussion at the kitchen table because money was scarce. Oftentimes, if a Black student does get the opportunity to attend a college or university, it is usually 1 out of every 10 students. A Black family of seven children would be lucky to have two or three of their children venture into higher education with those statistics.

Regardless of the reason, educational opportunities that some people take for granted others view as a true blessing. The prospect of graduating from a college or university means so much to a young Black boy or girl. It represents academic achievement, personal independence, financial freedom, wealth, and future prosperity. Having that type of opportunity is both life changing and rewarding. A college education is more than just having a piece of paper with your name on it from a university. It represents one's ability as a capable, competent, and productive member of society.

In spite of one's academic standing, college is a possibility for anyone willing to put in the time and effort to attend. Many public schools do not place emphasis on higher education in Black communities like they do in white communities. It is as if they want Blacks to believe that they do not have what it takes to succeed which is another one of the false narratives from our oppressors. Race is always an issue in this country. It does not matter what the topic or setting is, race will always emerge in the discussion. The objective here is to reject the negative and to move towards the positive.

In this case, the positive is to obtain a college education. We know that there will always be obstacles to overcome along the way because as Black Americans we are used to overcoming adversity in our lives. Half of the time it isn't even our families or society that holds us back from pursuing our academic dreams. Sometimes it is our own self-doubt that prevents us from attending college.

This is a fear I have witnessed with several of my former grade school students who were about to graduate from high school. They felt as though they didn't have what it takes to go to college. They assumed they needed a straight "A" average to be able to sustain at the university level. But I firmly reminded them that everyone is born intelligent and capable. The question is, what do we do with that knowledge?

Believe it or not, Black students do not need to have a perfect score on their Scholastic Assessment Test (SAT) or have a 4.0 grade point average (GPA) to get into the college or university of their choice. When I say, "The college or university of their choice," I do not mean what others have chosen for them. Some school counselors mislead our Black boys and girls by telling them that they do not qualify for certain colleges and universities, or that they are not smart enough.

In the words of James Baldwin, "I reject that Shit!" Someone can be an average student making average grades and qualify for college entrance. The opportunity for college choice is real because students pay for their college education. Either they work hard over the years in secondary school racking up thousands, if not hundreds of thousands of dollars in scholarship money, win a cash lottery, work a series of odd jobs saving every penny, apply for financial aid, or their family started a college fund for them at the time of their birth. Either way, regardless if a student comes from a lower class, middle class, or upper class family background the door to higher education is always open.

On that note, venturing into the college arena and representing that platform can be a huge undertaking. There are over five thousand colleges and universities within the United States alone. These higher education institutions range from community colleges offering associates degrees and certificates to Ivy League research institutions offering professional degrees. Depending on the college or university of choice, a student needs to consider which institution to apply to. If the student aspires to attend an Ivy League school, he or she should be mindful that there are eight Ivy League universities Black students should aim to attend if their academic career in grades k through 12 has effectively prepared them for the next stage in their educational journey. When choosing the college of your choice, go for the better option. Those universities include, but are not limited to the following:

1. Yale University
2. Harvard University
3. University of Pennsylvania
4. Brown University
5. Princeton University
6. Columbia University
7. Dartmouth University
8. Cornell University

However, if you want to take the historical route and attend one of the more prestigious Historically Black Colleges (HBCs) or Historically Black Universities (HBUs) located in the United States of America, look into those schools which have housed and educated some of our best and brightest Black Elite. There are ten highly prestigious Black colleges and Universities located in America which are known for producing celebrity and professional scholars. These higher education institutions instill within their students ideologies such as- self-reliance, educational excellence, professionalism, social justice, and economic empowerment.

When I think about famous Black people, I reflect on the ones who have positively and greatly impacted our race in a constructive and powerful way. I am not talking about self-serving individuals; I am speaking in regards to those who have truly made universal change. Those famous Black historians who have made a major difference in the world graduated from the following historically Black colleges and universities:

1. Martin Luther King: Morehouse College (Atlanta, GA)

2. Booker T. Washington: Hampton University (Hampton, VA)

3. Thurgood Marshall : Howard University (Washington, DC)

4. Jesse Jackson: North Carolina A & T University (Greensboro, NC)

5. Alice Walker: Spelman College (Atlanta, GA)

6. Ralph Waldo Ellison: Tuskegee University (Tuskegee, AL)

7. William B. Morris: Xavier University (New Orleans, LA)

8. James Weldon Johnson: Clark Atlanta University (Atlanta, GA)

9. W.E.B Du Bois and John Lewis: Fisk University (Nashville, TN)

10. John W. Thompson and Carrie Meek: FAMU (Tallahassee, FL)

Considering their individual triumphs, we know that the rigors of college life demands serious preparation. Therefore, in order to prepare for college, stay focused on your dreams, set realistic goals, commit to plenty of practice in regards to increasing math, reading, writing, thinking, and speaking skills. Learn how to manage your time well by donating enough time to the application process, three to four months should be sufficient time to devote to filling out and completing a series of college applications.

During this process, consider which colleges and universities are your main preferences. Be diligent and apply to those institutions. Incorporate all of your effective reading, writing, and vocabulary skills into these applications, and keep yourself well-rounded. This will allow you to explore your academic options during the college application process. Remember that adage, "Practice makes perfect." The more applications you complete the better your delivery, and the better your chances for being selected by those schools. If you challenge yourself, to get into the college or university of your choice through action, your dreams will come true.

Transitioning From High School to College

Most parents would say to their child, this is it. Now you are ready to go out in the world to explore, and to stake your claim in life. For the Black high school student this can be either an exciting or a frightening experience. The students I spoke with talked about their concerns regarding the transition from high school to college, especially during the application process. Several students were worried about their applications being rescinded until someone informed them that the application would not be revoked. A few students claimed that the admissions department at several colleges are "super chill" about grades, letting students know that grades are not the only consideration or factor in determining student acceptance into a college program. This news made most of them feel more at ease and confident about getting into the college of their choice.

However, several students were contemplating whether they have acquired enough high school credits to even be considered for college entrance. As parents working alongside our students on their academic journey, we must remember that high school is not necessarily a carefree and pleasant experience. This is the time when students are overwhelmed with high school courses they must pass in order to graduate and receive their high school diploma which is the metaphoric key to their future. They are also dealing with the personal, social, and emotional aspects of life. We, as the parent and life instructor, need to support them. That requires teaching your child how to cope with frustration, and how to minimize or eliminate their anxiety. Inform your child that colleges are evaluating the upward trend in their academic records over a course of time, and that the junior year in high school is rarely, or never a factor in this selection process. Moreover, make certain that your child has obtained the number of high school credits needed for college.

Even though high school is an enjoyable time for most students because it represents the final years of grade school, they need to be mindful of their academic competency levels and whether or not they have acquired enough transferrable credits for college. Students also need to be informed of the importance of their high school education moving forward as it represents the foundation for their college and professional careers. This leads me to question the motives of some high school counselors and administrators in urban education. Why is it that not all high schools place emphasis on higher education? Why are only a handful of Black boys and girls applying for college every year?

I remember when I attended high school. My counselors and administrators would always say, "Reach for the Stars," or "Dream Bigger." For me, that was positive support and encouragement. I remember those words even to this day. We must recognize that motivation is essential, especially for the 21st century Black student. However, as the main character in this scenario, the student also has to contribute to this process as well by being authentic in asking, "Am I really applying myself enough in each of my core classes?" If the answer is no, then the student needs to reflect on his or her actions and change the outcome to a positive result. It is understandable that leaving home to go to college, or attend a university miles away can be a frightening experience, but this is a journey everyone must take in order to procure educational and economic equity in life.

Family Influences

The family has the capacity to influence the choices students make regarding their future endeavors. Without even knowing it, a family member can encourage a student to make either the right or the wrong decision regarding college choice. Family members, especially parents, sometimes try to live vicariously through the life of their children. If there is something the parent neglected to pursue in his or her educational journey, the parent might project that experience on their child.

But, this is something that cannot be tolerated. The decision must be made by the student. It should never be a situation where the parent says, "Go to this college because I did okay," or "Your grandfather and uncle attended that university." Even though the parent may have their child's best interest at heart, the decision regarding college selection should remain in the hands of the high school student. Too often a student applies to colleges suggested by family members and not those colleges or universities they wanted to attend. Looking back on my own high school years, I see how the lack of family support and influence impeded my decision to go to college, and led me to attend colleges and universities of convenience instead of choice.

Now, as I help my own children prepare for higher education, I ponder on how my actions may influence their decisions as well. I understand the significance of the part I play as a parent. More importantly, I know that I must stress to my children that each of us are unified with a specific purpose and action in life. Even if we have different priorities and responsibilities, we each have the mutual belief and ability to succeed. Therefore, as a family unit, it is imperative to function at our most optimal efficiency, especially if we have a need to excel in both our academic and professional lives. It is through both education and positive family influences that we can make all of our dreams a reality. The mother and father are the ones who foster the norms and values for their child. For a student, the family name is the initial aspect of their identity. Moreover, the way in which the student represents his or her family name dictates how he or she feels about the family roots which are easily recognizable in the general public.

The Emotional Journey

There is an emotional aspect associated with attending a college or university. As a potential college student, one needs to evaluate the pros and cons of becoming a college resident. College is not for everyone. Some people just do not have the mentality level to attend a two year community college or a four year university.

College is extremely expensive, and it requires a lot of dedication and persistence. That is why it is imperative to consider the emotional aspect of attending college before actually taking that initial step.

This process involves understanding that your life is about to shift on a major level and to contemplate whether or not you are emotionally ready for the challenge. College is like a job. You cannot be absent from classes. You also have to be on time for each class every day and be ready to fully participate. If you do not attend your classes, you don't get paid. In college, you get paid in grades. You cannot afford to get poor grades unless you want to get kicked out of school. A college or university will place you on academic probation if your grades slip below a C-. That can really affect someone's emotional health, especially if he or she does not understand the politics involved in higher education. There are no excuses at the college level. Either you are emotionally prepared for the academic journey, or you are not.

In all seriousness, potential college students, especially Black students, need to have their minds right before venturing into higher education. When I attended junior college in Baltimore, there were always hundreds of students each year that would come to class for 2 or 3 weeks until they received their refund checks and then drop the class. It was crazy. They would just stop attending their classes. I recall having a discussion with my professor about how some people are not emotionally fit to attend college. He agreed by saying, "If the mind isn't right, you are not right!" Those words summed it up.

For the life of me, I could not understand why so many of my classmates stood in the registration line for over two hours, signed their signature to accept financial aid from the federal government, only to exit campus without a college degree. Obviously, they did not think about the long term benefit of obtaining a college education. When people allow their emotions to take over, they react to situations impulsively. There is no thinking or planning involved in their actions. In life you cannot just go around acting on impulse, you have to think before you act. If someone wants to attend a college or a university, that person needs to realize that attending a higher education institution demands focus and commitment.

Needless to say, our emotional well-being is an essential part of our mindset as it applies to adjusting to college life. For most people who register for college, the goal is to obtain educational and economic equity. Those are the ones who comprehend the purpose for higher learning at the college and university level. They understand the significance and value in obtaining a college degree. There are no distorted views regarding their reasons for attending college. They view college as the gateway to their future.

Moreover, their minds are in the right emotional state because they have a plan, and they are ready to follow through. I am not saying that college is easy, or that there will not be any roadblocks along the way. I am merely saying that before you decide to attend college make certain you are able to go all the way. If you are not ready for that type of commitment, take another path in life. Otherwise, you will regret it in the end. But, if you feel as though you have what it takes, and you know you can go the distance, do it. Just remember that going to college is a serious decision and a major step that requires time, energy, and dedication, so if you are in the right frame of mind go for it. If not, save your money and don't waste your time.

The Spiritual Journey

Some people may ask, what does religion have to do with college? I say to them everything. When you are a first time college student without a car, you have to depend on public transportation to get to and from school. You cannot imagine how many times I prayed traveling to and from college campus on a daily basis. I basically feared for my life. For me it was a dangerous situation. There were drug dealers and drug addicts at nearly every bus stop I waited on. For some unknown reason, most of the colleges and universities in Maryland are located near danger zones. Half of these campuses are located in West Baltimore while the other campuses are located in East Baltimore.

Believe me when I say, I am not disrespecting Baltimore. I grew up in the city, but there were no drug dealers and drug addicts lurking in my neighborhood. I lived down the street from Ernie Boston of FOX 45 News, and around the corner from Oprah Winfrey when she worked for WJZ News 13. That seems like a lifetime ago now. But, the reality is that when I started going to college the streets of Baltimore began to get somewhat suspect. I remember praying before I left home for school, while riding the number 13 bus, and once I got off of the bus to cross the street to enter the college campus.

In all honesty, this is my truth. I cannot speak for other people, but I can reflect on my own college experiences. Luckily for me I was already a member of a church, and I believed in a higher power. If it wasn't for my religious beliefs and my faith in God, I dare to imagine what my life could have been like without my spiritual background. There is an adage that says, God helps those who help themselves. I truly believe that if someone works hard enough and stays focused he or she will succeed in life.

Furthermore, I believe that we are the makers of our own destiny in conjunction with our spiritual faith in God. Everything we have in life and who we become as parents and professionals are a blessing from God. There are some people in this world who praise themselves and others for their accomplishments and material wealth. I give my thanks to the Lord Jesus Christ. Whenever I found myself in a challenging situation in college, I would give that situation to God. That allowed me to stay focused and to ignore the madness around me during that time in my life. Even at the college level, you will be confronted with people who try to hold you back or create conflict to distract you from your goals. But, you have to reject the foolishness, and remain steadfast on your academic journey.

Despite what others may say regarding my journey, I know that my spiritual relationship with God got me through all of the difficult times I encountered along the way. College was rough for me in the beginning, not because of the courses I took, that was the easy part, but because of the unprofessional and ignorant people I encountered along the way. In college, if you are too knowledgeable people hate you, and if you are too quiet they try you. Focusing on man made conflicts and chaos is a waste of time because it is futile and ineffectual.

On the other hand, embracing your spiritual faith in times of challenge and great peril is a more effective use of your time and energy. Knowing who we are in the world has a lot to do with our comfort and ability level in life. Once you have established your identity in life, no one can take anything away from you. There is a quote in Hebrews 11:1 of the Bible that says, "Now faith is the assurance of things hoped for, the conviction of things not seen," regardless if we can see these things or not, we know that all of these things are possible due to having a religious foundation and relationship with God. Even Dr. Martin Luther King, Malcolm X, and the Obama's held to their religious beliefs throughout the course of their lives. The spiritual relationship we all have with God is our sanctity. That is what gives us the strength and the endurance we need to persevere in this complex and corrupt world.

Identity Influences

Knowing who I am in the world in regards to being a Black American, someone's child, a mother, a sibling, an aunt, a cousin, a student for life, a professional, and most importantly a capable human being, I see how my projected image of self has led to my college choices or lack thereof. But, I am always cognizant and mindful of the fact that how I view my self-worth and self-value in this world can be projected on my children. Keeping this in mind, I consciously reject any negative characterizations placed upon me or my race. The concept of identity relates to how I view myself as a unique individual. In that regard, I perceive myself as a confident, knowledgeable, assertive, diligent, friendly, kind, and generous person. These are some of the characteristics that define me as a human being. I further understand that what I think about myself and how I feel about myself can be either positively or negatively interpreted by others.

On that note, who we are and how we feel about ourselves can influence our decisions in life which mostly stems from our own self-perception. Knowledge of our identity is a contributing factor to how we connect with others. It demonstrates our academic and intellectual competencies as well as our predispositions towards education. Our tendency to make decisions regarding college choice is usually based on our attitudes about learning and our desire for success. The college or university we select has to be a higher education institution we can connect with on various levels. To all intents and purposes, most higher learning institutions, colleges and universities, captivate potential students with their mission and vision statement. It is a powerful and persuasive statement because it establishes a deeply rooted connection with those pursuing higher education, especially when the mission and vision statements resonate with our own belief system.

Historically White Colleges and Universities (HWCUs) versus Historically Black Colleges and Universities (HBCUs)

When we hear the terms HWCU and HBCU, we think about historically white colleges and universities and historically black colleges and universities. We also ponder about the color of success, and the price for meeting that academic and professional goal. This makes the average person wonder, will I become more successful in life graduating from a white university, or from a black university? One may even question, is one university paradigm more prevalent than the other, or is it all an illusion? There are a series of dynamics which differentiate HWCUs from HBCUs and vice versa.

Those similarities and differences are distinctive in nature based on race, pedigree, history, alumni and general location. With that in mind, historically white universities are deeply rooted in plantation politics with a disproportionality of Black students accepted into their academic programs and higher learning institutions whereas HBCUs have a clearly defined open-door policy for whites and other non-Black students. The differentials between these two organizations are indisputably evident in the real-world. For instance, for every graduating class of students from a predominantly Black high school, only two or three students from that graduating class of seniors are accepted into a predominantly white university. Although race is not the only distinction between these two college communities, it is the most prevalent of issues regarding student acceptance into HWCUs.

Ideally, Black students with exceptional grade point averages (GPAs) would be viewed as an asset to any four year college or university regardless of their race, pedigree, or socioeconomic background. These are students who have excelled at every level of their academic career during grade school. However, we live in the real world where race, pedigree, and one's background is a determinant regarding their entry into a predominantly white university, especially those institutions founded on plantation politics.

Historically speaking, there have been multiple predominantly white universities known for broadcasting racist white supremacy propaganda such as white students uttering racist tirades on college campuses, making racial slurs, writing racist graffiti on the walls of university campuses, posting racist videos on school websites, or inciting racial hate crimes against Black students attending their universities. For most Black potential college students, these types of actions would be an immediate deterrent from attending a predominantly white university. But, students who want to attend any college of their choice may find this type of adversity as a minor challenge. In spite of the circumstance, students do have the right to attend any college they aspire to as potential college students, and they have the ability to persevere in their efforts as future professionals.

Unfortunately, predominantly white universities in the United States continue to practice plantation politics on their college campuses which incites fear. These types of politics cause great danger for many Americans, especially the Black American male or female attempting to join a predominantly white higher education institution. If a university only focuses on a specific interest group, it is not a united force for the people. Instead, it is operating as a separatist organization. Moreover, this is an organization that is not based on the fundamental principles which focus on the protections and rights of all races and creeds of people.

Unfortunately, plantation politics continue to encourage disproportionality and inequality outcomes at the university level which negatively impact professional career and income ratios for Black Americans. The promotion of racial degradation breeds inside the predominantly white universities only cater to the needs of their own race. They oppose affirmative action and devalue people of color and their cultural heritage. To this day, some white universities continue to cater to non-Black interest groups that are opposed to the Black Lives Matter Movement and more interested in white power. This is an obvious example of the great divide in American society at the higher education level.

On the other side of that spectrum are the historically black colleges and universities which cater to all who enter their college campuses. Historically, the first HBCUs were established in Pennsylvania and Ohio way before the American Civil War. During that time period, Blacks were not allowed to attend predominantly white colleges or universities due to race. Black colleges and universities were founded to provide Blacks with comprehensive skills to help them become professional tradesmen and educators.

Today, HBCUs provide students with a plethora of college majors and programs to prepare students for future careers in the workforce. In contrast to the white college experience for Black students, the student experience for non-Black students attending these colleges and universities has always been welcoming and positive. Black colleges and universities have an open-door policy that invites all races to attend their higher education institutions.

These colleges and universities are principled on promoting culture, heritage, unity, and pride. Unlike predominantly white colleges and universities, historically Black colleges and universities bridge relationships within its campus community based on respect and brotherhood. Students view each other as being valued members of the college learning environment. These colleges and universities oppose division, and support unity among its college family members. Furthermore, the historically

Black college and university is known for creating a beacon of hope for those who may not have been able to obtain a professional degree at a predominantly white college or university.

Both historically white colleges and universities and historically black colleges and universities focus on the well-being and success of its student population. These institutions are embedded on historical beliefs and practices which are deeply rooted and based on individual preferences unique to their student population. Both of these institution types are grounded in a mission and vision uniquely affiliated to the premise of its founding fathers. The initial erection of these colleges and universities were based on the racial divide which continues to be a contributing factor in modern day higher education.

Furthermore, the premise for establishing white and black colleges and universities was to enhance the socioeconomic advancement of the people in each subgroup although it was not a unified or collective process. Regardless, the division between the historically white colleges and universities and the historically black colleges and universities, both serve a purpose in American society as it applies to economic productivity for this nation. Keep in mind that if a Black student decides to attend a HWCU or a HBCU; their educational success will still benefit the population as a whole regarding government tax revenue.

In the end, every student attending a college or university in the United States of America becomes a tax number, regardless of race, creed, or social status. It does not matter if you were born rich or poor. You will always be paying taxes once you matriculate from college into the workforce. The real questions to consider are, what are you the student looking to learn from the institution of your choice, and what is it that you want from this higher learning institution? If you can answer these questions, you are that much closer to making your college choice decision.

Keep in mind that the big picture is your future. Your final decision is less about the institution itself, and more about what you plan on doing with the rest of your life. Too often people make the wrong decision regarding their career choices based on immediate need, pressure from their family, or suggestions from their friends. Make certain that you have some sort of interest in the major you decide to venture into and the college you apply to for academic and training purposes. You do not want to waste valuable time participating in and paying for a college program you are not interested in pursuing after graduation.

The Final Decision

If someone told you that making your final college decision would be a simple task, that person lied to you. The college decision making process is anything but easy. It requires a great deal of deliverance, management, determination, direction, control, and judgment on behalf of the decision maker. The scope of the "college decision making process" is extensive to say the least. As a potential college or university student, deciding on what path to take can be both an exhausting and overwhelming venture. Don't get me wrong, I know how exciting making that final decision can be when deciding on which college or university to attend. I just mean it is a complicated task. That is why it is so important to have that family support.

Everyone can use some guidance here and there. As a family, I encourage you to take a tour of the college campus with your high school senior to get a feel for the college community. Decide if you can envision yourself functioning within that college campus. Your child should be able to ask him or herself, do I feel an immediate connection with the people and this environment, or do I see myself as being part of this particular learning community? If the answer is yes, you are that much closer to making that final decision, but if the answer is no, there is more work to be done.

Moving forward, with any decision in life requires self-reflection. You need to assess your options and bring everything into focus, and pay attention to every detail. Evaluate and analyze the situation if necessary. By asking, what do I think about the mission and vision of this learning institution? How do I feel about attending this college or university? Does this higher learning institution have the college major I am interested in, and what does this school have to offer me as a young Black student?

Knowing what you are looking for in a college will help you make that final decision. Therefore, on this self-reflecting journey, you as the potential college student must be prepared to make some difficult decisions along the way regarding your future.

In life, your verdict towards educational and economic equity derives from your commitment. As you ponder on which road to travel during your college journey, know that you can make this academic process an adventure, or it can become an incubus of your own making. This leads me to a few final questions regarding college choice such as: am I applying to this university because my best friend and boyfriend attend this school? Am I applying to this college because of their impressive medical school, engineering department, and business program, or am I just fascinated by the aesthetics? Just know you should always be able to identify with your college or university of choice on some concrete or superficial level. Basically, make certain that beyond any doubt you are choosing the school that is best for you, and you alone because this is a new chapter in your life.

Children attending grade school are often asked, on several different occasions in various grades, what do you want to be when you grow up? As trivial as that question may seem, it does serve a viable and significant purpose. While some children respond to that question immediately without hesitation, many of them remain quiet or perplexed. As a reserved and shy child, not willing to share my thoughts at that particular moment in my life, I did not know what I wanted to be at that young age. For the most part, I guess when we are children we are too busy playing with our toys, hanging out with our friends and neighbors, or daydreaming about life to contemplate on adult matters from a child's perspective. Now that I reflect on those childhood days, I wish I would have put more energy and thought into the philosophical question, what do you want to be in life? But, that time has passed, and now I am an adult already settled in my life. Thanks to my aunts and uncles and brothers and sisters I realized what I had to do with my life, and I made a choice to go to college and major in an area that would benefit both me and my family.

As time moved on, I began taking courses at Baltimore City Community College in Baltimore, Maryland. From there, I proceeded to extend my academic career by attending and graduating from Coppin State College for undergrad and graduate school. I worked several odd jobs to pay my way through college. I never believed in accumulating unnecessary financial debt. I guess you can say that I was extremely driven to succeed. I was just a young Black woman trying to make a living for herself and her family. Even then, I was still uncertain about my actual professional path in life, but I knew I had to do something fruitful and productive, so that I could provide for my family. I always put my family first. You see, when you are responsible for others, you tend to put childish things behind you as you look towards the future. Although some would say that the future is uncertain, I am a firm believer in making my dreams a reality. I used to tell my own children, either you make a life for yourself, or life will make one for you. The latter is the negative you want to avoid by all means. However, due to my self-motivation, high self-esteem, and my self-sufficient attitude in life, I was able to attend and graduate from Loyola University in Maryland and Morgan State University with honors. Those were some of the monumental events in my life.

After enhancing and crafting one's specialty skills at the higher education level, college graduates seek job opportunities that will solidify their academic journey to become successful, competent, and lifelong professional workers. One's intellectual knowledge, vocational training, management of time, and leadership skills contribute to whether or not he or she is prepared and ready to transition into the professional world. At this point in time, some people are skeptical about the career journey while others are confident and self-assured in the talents and skills learned at the university level. However, one thing college graduates rarely seem to contemplate when seeking employment is the issue regarding income inequality. For decades, people of color have been paid less than other races occupying the same career title or position. There continues to be a racial gap wage in the United States. Even today Asian, white, and Latino

Americans have the highest median wages compared to Blacks who are ranked among those ethnic groups receiving the lowest median wage.

Yet, as a race, we should not be surprised about those occupational disparities because this has been going on since slavery, the Black man not being compensated for his worth. Therefore, when we think about our professional careers, we must keep in mind that, "Negroes, traditionally the last to be hired and the first to be fired, are finding jobs harder to get..." (Baldwin, 1984, p. 42). Today Blacks continue to be marginalized for their work ethic. There is a bitter expectancy we as Americans have when we follow the norms, but are denied our financial reward. Regardless of race, everyone is entitled to receive fair consideration for employment, and appropriate and equitable compensation for their work. People should not be looked over for certain positions because of race, but unfortunately that is a reality Blacks experience when seeking career positions in spite of their educational background and professional capabilities.

Assess Yourself

The first step on the road to obtaining a professional career is to conduct a self-assessment. This process entails determining your value as a potential employee or partner in a company. Making any important decisions in life requires us to always evaluate ourselves. This means to know who you are and what you are capable of doing. Start by asking yourself, what am I good at? What are some skills I possess that will help me land this job? What do I need to brush up on? Do I have enough experience for this career paying job? How can I contribute to this company? These are just a few questions which come to mind during the job seeking process. Be aware that your values describe who you are because those elements represent your true personal identity. Know your work related values, your personal interests, preferences, and professional ideals in an effort to prepare yourself before the actual interview.

When all is said and done, it will be the time and effort you put into assessing your skill set that would have assisted you in obtaining the job you desire. That is why it is imperative that your assessment of self is thorough and accurate. Before the interview process, you want to make certain that you have covered your bases. Potential employers usually conduct the interview with a series of self-evaluative questions to ascertain the interviewee's competency levels. For instance, you may be asked, what are your strengths? What are your weaknesses? Why do you want this job? Where would you like to be in your career five years from now, and my favorite question, what attracted you to this company? This is always an excellent and beneficial exercise to use to help you prepare for the actual event, so thinking about your professional expectations and capabilities now will benefit you in the long run.

Identify Your Innate Skill Sets

I remember when I was a little girl; I used to see my neighbor Mr. Bivens driving his Verizon truck to and from work everyday. I wondered what it would be like to work for the telephone company. Mr. Bivens always had a smile on his face and his wife and kids seemed so happy. I guess you can say I was inspired. One day I got up the nerve to ask my neighbor if he liked his job, and what were some of his professional responsibilities. He informed me that to become a telephone technician I would have to know about installation and maintenance repair in addition to a sequence of other skill sets which I did not possess at the time being a 13 year old. Needless to say, Mr. Bivens responses to my questions gave me pause. He actually gave me something to think about in reference to my future professional career choices. I knew that I loved to sing, and perform short acting performances in front of my family. I liked playing school with my younger siblings, and I always enjoyed drawing and writing poems. This was my starting point.

In reality I knew that working for the telephone company was not for me because I never demonstrated a desire to venture into that career field. Moving forward, I knew I needed to be honest and authentic with myself about my career aspirations. Even at such a young age it was necessary for me to reflect on both my natural talents and my academic skills. Math, reading, and writing were my favorite subjects in grade school. I even enjoyed learning about Early American and World History. However, being Black, I was also familiar with "The Black Tax" which continues to be a systemic issue for working class Black Americans. In spite of what career path I decided to choose, I knew I had to be the best of the best in order to become successful in any profession. However, I for one believe in my professional competency levels as a human being. Ergo, in the final analysis, it is your personality that will get you the job, but it is your innate skill ability that will help you keep the job.

Testing Your Skill Sets

If you want to confirm your intellectual knowledge regarding your skill ability levels, apply what you have learned on your academic journey from grade school to college to your career. Let's face it; we all have transferable skill abilities that are not related to any one particular job which can benefit us regardless of the career we choose in life. Several of us have effective social, artistic, creative, and technical skills while others struggle in these skill areas. That would be your innate abilities or your individual capabilities as a potential employee for any business or organization. In fact, these skill sets are general abilities pertaining to our own basic instincts. We usually identify these skills as transferable skills because we utilize these skills to adapt to any given situation whenever we need to persevere and demonstrate our competency level in a particular career field or profession. For many of us, this entails being able to demonstrate effective leadership and communication skills in the workplace by establishing oneself as an effective speaker and director in an administrative role. Others view these skill sets as having the ability to analyze, evaluate, and interpret information clearly while modeling critical thinking skills as an organizational leader. Keep in mind that regardless of your career path, you have the internal skills to help you "fake it until you make it."

From a professional perspective, not allowing yourself to self-evaluate your academic skills and professional training knowledge will place you in an awkward position within the workforce. Your colleagues are always watching you and you will be expected to contribute to the group as a valued and competent team member. Therefore, it is your responsibility to be ready to lead. It is far better to be prepared for the unexpected on the job, then to be confronted with the unexpected and not being prepared. Our skill knowledge is our preparation for any workplace situation which may or may not arise during the duration of our employment. In other words, I would rather have the knowledge and not need it instead of needing to know something, and being completely lost. In retrospect, the skills I acquired from grade school such as writing techniques, mathematical competency, and developing my social skills have prepared me for both my college and professional career. I am so appreciative of the teachers who worked with me during my adolescent years leading to my final days of high school. They have instilled within me a work ethic which I continue to reflect upon and utilize every day. Thanks to my former teachings, I have greatly benefited as a professional, and I continue to enhance my academic, technical, and social skill abilities each year I instruct my own students.

In all reality, your skill base is what gets you the job, but your ability to utilize those skills effectively and purposefully will help you keep your position. In turn, there are a series of questions we tend to ask ourselves while contemplating our ability levels as potential employees such as, what skills do I feel competent about? Which skills do I most enjoy demonstrating in a group, and what skills demonstrate my lack of competency? For each of these three questions, there are a variety of possible answers to satisfy each of the statements. However, as we continue to reflect upon our competency levels and evaluate our skill sets, we further need to self-analyze what we know and what we need to learn to better position ourselves for the workforce. For instance, you should develop a brief work survey to determine your competency levels for a specific career or occupation. Make certain that your line of questioning uniquely caters to that particular career knowledge base. Be mindful that each career has a different set of expectations regarding skill ability level and intellectual functionality. For the average person, this process involves evaluating one's comfort level with explaining things to people, interpreting and critiquing information, understanding workplace policies and politics, being able to advise and collaborate with others, having an ability to manage time wisely by self-managing your own skills, and being attuned to current workplace paradigms regarding organizational productivity.

Professional Career Choices

Even though we previously discussed the relevance for self-assessing your skill sets, keep in mind that your career options will vary based on your skill ability level. That is why it is important to make the correct decisions when seeking a specific career field. This is not something anyone should venture into blindly, but with an open mind. There are several questions you need to ask yourself such as: do I have the appropriate skill set for this career position? Am I adequately prepared to do the job, and what are the essential skills I need to be able to do the job effectively? Your responses to these questions will demonstrate your readiness level for the job. On any given day, someone may claim to be prepared for any job, but the reality is, either you have the qualifying skills or you don't. Hopefully, you have prepared yourself well enough to not only get the job, but to keep the job. The goal is to be the best of the best. People who demonstrate essential skills and effective traits regarding work ethic are the ones who are most admired in the workplace. They are highly respected and highly regarded as field experts because of their unique skill sets. That is the mindset one must have when pursuing a professional career paying job because if you have the ability you will be hired for the position.

As I mentioned before, please take the time to determine your fit for the job you seek. Potential employees do their homework by researching their career of choice. This is called "doing the footwork." You need to know the responsibilities and mechanics associated with the position. You will also want to know the monetary, stock, and health benefits offered with the hiring package in addition to the work hours. Moreover, evaluating the pros and cons associated with the job is a necessity as well. Please consider all of the above before making the final career choice. It is essential for you to make the right decision so you can avoid working in a career you do not enjoy. Remember, this is a professional commitment. All too often, people accept jobs they have nothing in common with just for the money. Despite what the career is you should always have a passion to work in that particular field. If the connection is not there, the happiness on the job will not last for long. Then, you may become extremely bitter and miserable on the job. You want to ensure that the career decision you make is something you enjoy and love. Otherwise, you may have lifelong regret.

On a happier note, despite the current situation with the job market, there are plenty of professional positions available to all who choose to apply. Knowing that the fourth industrial workforce revolution is among us we must be adamant in our pursuit of quality employment. We want to be compensated for our talents and skills as potential employees. In that, we must consider our worth and value as an asset for any company or organization when applying for a career position. The two questions you should ask yourself are, what does this business have to offer me, and how can I contribute to this company as a potential employee? Take the necessary time to respond to those questions before signing your name on the dotted line. See the bigger picture. You are your own valuable resource, so make things happen for you and your family. Always make decisions based on your professional and personal beliefs, and consider what is best for you. Reject any negativity in the atmosphere. There are a plethora of career opportunities for everyone willing to take a risk on their own dreams and aspirations in life. You are the director of your own destiny, so do not allow others to dictate your future. Make things happen for yourself because you are a competent and capable human being. There are so many professional opportunities waiting for you. You just have to decide on the career of your choice.

Decide on a Career or Occupation

Should I become an investment banker, a comedian, a surgeon, an architect, or an actor? These are a few occupations I considered along the way during my pilgrimage as a young adult, so many choices and not enough time. Time is money, and money is time. I recall hearing that phrase often throughout my lifetime. But, I never really placed emphasis on its meaning or relevance in the professional world until I became a professional myself. Working a 9 to 5, you come to realize and appreciate the value of time which leads to the outcome being money. In the workforce one does not exist without the other. These two concepts are interchangeable. That is why deciding on the right career choice is an essential aspect to obtaining financial sustainability. A job pays an employee at an hourly rate, whereas a career compensates an employee with an annual salary. Sometimes people select careers they find doable, but the reality is that the choice should be based on your long term goals like raising a family and buying a home.

Needless to say, I did not choose any of those professions that I mentioned initially. Instead, I became a school teacher, not by choice but out of necessity. Anyone with children will tell you that when you have a family the goal is to get the job, to obtain some sort of financial stability, and get paid. It is not about being selective in your choices, especially if you have a family to support. But, for the college graduate straight out of school, you do have options because you are your only responsibility. On that note, decide on a career in which you can see yourself doing long term. Go for a career that resonates with your character and professional objectives. Consider everything you learned during your academic career that has led you to this juncture in your life. Do not opt for a career because most Black people work in that particular field. Do not be afraid to think outside the box. Trust your knowledge and your instincts, and most of all believe in yourself. Reject any limitations the world or you may place in your path. Once you reach a final decision regarding your career choice, proceed to applying for the job. Always remember you have what it takes to succeed.

Conduct Informational Interviews

After you have conducted an interview self-assessment, identified your innate skill sets, and decided on a specific career path, now it is time to proceed with the actual interview. Dress professionally, keep your composure, and remember to introduce yourself. When the interviewee is on the frontline of an interview, he or she often becomes nervous about the entire situation, oftentimes asking him or herself in a humorous way, what the hell am I doing here? Most of the time the answer is to earn a paycheck, but that should never be the main reason why we seek employment. This is not just a job. It is more than that. This is your future. Moreover, this is the beginning of the rest of your life as an adult. With that being said, you should always focus on your true passion. For example, if you like taking pictures of landscapes and people, become a photographer, not a chef. If you like saving lives, become a medical doctor. Whatever your career decision, the interview process establishes your preparedness for that particular occupation. While you may believe you are a perfect fit, the interviewer may not find you suitable for the position.

Ironically, as you sit there across from your potential employer, you notice that you never seem to ask the right questions before accepting the job. This is a major mistake because it can lead to disappointment and regret in the long run. But if you pose the right questions, you can save yourself from decades of heartache and professional regret. Think of that moment as an informational interview. You are there to provide and gather information regarding the career of your choice. It does not matter if the interviewer is black or white. Your main objective is to sell yourself. No one knows you better than you know yourself. Dig deep within yourself and retrieve that self-confidence, self-recognition, self-value, and self-worth to convince the company manager that you are the right person for the job. Represent yourself as being a competent and valuable asset for any organization. When you believe what you are saying about yourself, they start to believe in you as a potential employee. Never underestimate who you are during a job interview because self-doubt is not attractive, and it definitely is not hirable.

Get that Job

Now is the time to obtain the job you desire. Rely on the people within your community to assist you on your employment journey. You do not have to do this alone. If you need someone to coach you before you apply for the job or schedule an interview, do that. It is best to be prepared for employment opposed to being unprepared. Finding and maintaining a career paying job is essential to human survival. Nothing in life is free. We need financial resources to sustain ourselves throughout the course of our lives. There are many monetary constants in life such as paying for gas and electric, paying a water bill, housing, transportation to and from work, medical, health, and life insurance, clothing and food. Without a dependable source of income it is difficult for people to live comfortably. Therefore, if you want the job, put forth the effort. Don't procrastinate, just go for it. Believe in yourself and in your abilities. Remember that you have what it takes to succeed. We all must keep in mind that in the Black community, we have to promote financial independence through career attainment. Each one of us must be willing to teach others how to get the job and keep the job. These types of selfless acts will definitely help our community members advance themselves intellectually and professionally.

In spite of the competition you may encounter while applying for a career paying job, you have to be assertive in your ability to get the job. The only thing really standing between you and a job is your attitude and comfort level. When you are sitting across from a potential employer during an interview, he or she can sense your nervousness, see the uncertainty in your facial expression, and hear the lack of confidence in your voice. So, be confident in your approach for the job. Avoid displaying any signs of precariousness, skepticism, or incertitude. What you need to do is appear calm, cool, and collective by demonstrating self-reliance and self-assurance in your innate abilities as a potential employee for any company or organization. This is the moment you have been working towards. You have worked hard for many years by obtaining the appropriate education and getting the necessary training for this position. Now is not the time for self-doubt. This is the time to address the difficult questions early on and prepare yourself for your professional journey. Make certain you are in the right frame of mind by remaining positive and professional. Think to yourself, "I got this!" Positive thoughts and positive energy always bring about positive results.

Even today, the decision you make will impact the rest of your life, so be courageous enough to go through the process of getting your just rewards. Sometimes when it comes to getting the career job we have been dreaming about we have doubts about our skill abilities. We often become our worst critics by questioning, am I good enough for the job? Do I have what it takes, or is there someone better who might get the job instead? Thinking those types of thoughts are counterproductive, and create a domino effect. Instead of getting the job, you will end up causing yourself to go against what you are actually trying to achieve in life. Being Black, the world is already against you. So, do not create a self-destructive mindset. Remain positive at all times even when faced with adversity. You will receive the extrinsic motivation you need from friends and family members, but the intrinsic motivation is something you have to build within yourself. That is the self-motivation piece that we all rely upon to get us through the most challenging and darkest hours of our lives. You do this by surrounding yourself with positive people and keeping a positive mindset. This is your opportunity to shine. You are the master of your professional journey, and you have what it takes to steer the course of your career path.

Another thing, don't take no for an answer. Throughout the duration of both your academic and professional journey the aim has always been to obtain and establish educational and economic equity. Knowing that the two entities go hand and hand, you must be steadfast in your pursuit to reach your ultimate goals. Everyone has his or her own personal, professional, and financial aspirations in life. The commonality between us all is the need to achieve those dreams. Before we had goals, we had aspirations which are basically things we aspire to accomplish on our individual pilgrimage. The objective we aim towards in our efforts and deeds determine the end result of our academic and professional journey. Either we target our desired result with forceful, intentional, meaningful, purposeful, ambitious, and vigorous drive, or we just settle for what life places at our feet. Even though the decision is yours, try to advocate for yourself by taking the initiative to achieve your intended success. In all honesty, college is not for everyone. Maybe you took another path like classes at a career training or technical school. Regardless of the professional path you took to get to this juncture in your life, now is the time to take that final step to securing long term employment and income stability.

Build Your Career

If you are in this career for the long term, start building up your momentum to keep the job. Start by thinking about long term objectives. Begin this process by asking yourself the following questions, where do I see myself in five years? What do I need to do to become a manager or corporate partner in this firm? These are basic questions to help drive your ambition and keep you focused on future successes in your career. Since we are living in a technological world, you know you are going to have to learn new skills and expand your knowledge on technological platforms, interfaces and programs. While gaining management experience, you should work towards improving your communication and management skills. Be strategic in your efforts by developing a career plan and stick with it. Also, utilize your time wisely and increase your efficiency rates to complete projects. This will definitely make you stand out from your colleagues and your supervisor will take notice. At this point, it is about proving yourself to be a valuable asset for the company. Accountability and reliability are always impressive assets to demonstrate in the workforce if you want to be recognized for higher level positions. Progression would be the next step within that 5 year duration of employment.

To put it bluntly, you really need to focus on making a change that will not only open doors for you, but will benefit the young Black youth coming behind you as well. Your actions can create a counteraction that will either open doors for young Black males and females, or it will close that professional door on them forever. In most professions the ratio of black to white professionals is unequal. More than seventy-five percent of the career paying workforces has been monopolized by white Americans. That may sound surreal, but it is a current reality in the job market. As we already know this is another example of professional and financial inequality in this country as it pertains to race. I don't have to explain the concept of racism to you because we all have unfortunately experienced it at some point in our lives. During my naive years as a Black youth, I recall watching the news or a sitcom seeing Blacks mistreated and thinking to myself, "That won't happen to me." But, it did happen to me on several occasions throughout the course of my life. It happened at a department store, in grade school, at a HBCU and at a HWCU, and ironically during my teaching career by white colleagues and black supervisors. In spite of all of the foolishness on the job, you have to decide. It is either going to be you or them. This is when your spiritual education comes into play. With that being said, just give the madness to God and keep it moving, and do not allow anyone to destroy everything you have worked so hard to build. Remember, the devil is a liar!

In all honesty, the only way we can ensure educational and economic equity outcomes for our families and for our Black race in general is to take action now. It is great to protest in the streets about social injustice, police brutality, unfair treatment, and the lack of educational and employment opportunities for Blacks, but there are so much more we need to do as a race. When I am teaching on the job, I think about the big picture by asking myself, "How many Black boys and girls can I help to make college and career ready?" This is in spite of the social injustice and push back I may encounter in my career because in the forefront of my mind, I am constantly thinking about contributing to the Black community as a whole.

If everyone in the Black race understood that our journey is not actually singled but it is paired, we could greatly alter the present reality we as a race are currently experiencing in America. There is a way to change our current academic and professional situation in this world. Either we take action and just focus on ourselves individually, or we look at the broader purpose for our lives. In the introduction, the question I posed was what is our purpose in life? Is it to live a selfish existence or to live a fruitful one by helping our fellow Black community members excel as well? Essentially our professional standing in an organization or company can become beneficial for the entire Black community not just for our own family. Remember the slogan, "Each one teaches one." That is why it is so important to position ourselves in these companies and organizations. Then, we can give someone else a hand up, instead of a handout.

Professional Careers are Not Professional

Ideally when we hear the phrase "professional career," we indulge in the idea of a picturesque career pathway. Often we have visions of a perfect workplace environment where everyone is seen, heard, and respected as valuable members of the professional team. We even have ideals of being treated fairly as colleagues, but that is not always the reality. Within this workforce paradigm exists two separate realities. Those realities are either professionalism or unprofessionalism taking place in the work environment. In fact, some workplaces are consumed with racial inequality that restricts the Black race from advancing quickly up the chain of command, while others have Blacks in leadership roles that have an "Uncle Tom" mentality causing them to condemn their own race.

These companies, with their unethical leadership practices, continue to devalue the Black employee by ignoring the Black man's worth. In America, companies or businesses claim to be working towards developing a racially just work place, but those are just false narratives.

Those companies are failing the Black employee by denying them professional advancement opportunities within their corporations. Booker T. Washington once said, "Success is to be measured not so much by the position that one has reached in life as by the obstacles which one has overcome while trying to succeed." There is a slippery slope between obtaining a career paying job and keeping it, especially when there are forces within your base trying to destroy your professional career.

In this 21st century employment paradigm, there is an obvious disconnect within the work environment. Supervisors are abusing their authority by mistreating staff members, and many people are experiencing stress due to the unprofessionalism they encounter from colleagues and administrators. This type of tension impacts productivity levels within the workplace and creates massive conflict. When we take a deep look into how Black Americans are faring in the workforce, we see that they are not doing well compared to their white counterparts. It seems as though supervisors are becoming more and more critical towards their Black staff, and Black staff members are becoming more and more withdrawn from the work community.

This creates an environment where employees become skeptical of their supervisors, and the bond of trust is broken. It is difficult to work in an environment where you cannot trust the people you work with due to their unethical and corrupt practices. Instead of harassing Blacks and undervaluing their contributions to the workforce, these supervisors need to appreciate the genius and creativity Black Americans bring to any organization. It is the absence of trust and the presence of inequality within the workplace that creates the false narrative called professionalism.

On the other end of that spectrum, most people try to ignore the inequalities which exist in the workplace because they are living in denial. They can care less about the politics taking place in the work environment. For them, it is just another day on the job. They accept the madness happening around them as being the norm, or they are too afraid of losing their jobs to complain. I can remember several occasions when I was harassed by my supervisor at different work locations. It was a living nightmare. That is why I moved from school to school. Their actions were always personal and never professional. I don't believe they even knew the definition of the word "professionalism." That common word seemed foreign to them. For the average supervisor, the workplace is their personal playground, and believe me when I say, "They play dirty."

If you are more educated than them and have more letters behind your name, they try to destroy you by breaking your spirit. Moreover, if you dress better than them and seem happier and more put together, they will definitely try to demolish you. Luckily for me I have a strong formal, informal, and spiritual educational background. Otherwise, I probably would have quit like some of my former colleagues. On occasion, my former peers and I would vent about the madness which took place Monday through Friday on the job. Sometimes we would call each other on the weekend to discuss the craziness happening in our workplace. I always found the practice of venting to colleagues to be a healthy release system from the chaos and unprofessionalism that exist on the job. Being a focused individual, I keep in mind that my job is my livelihood, and I try not to allow the devil to rob me of the time and hard work I put into my professional career.

However, for the most part, this is something that can be rectified with community support and precision to create long lasting change in the work environment. In the ideal world, administrators and staff would be respectful of one another. Administrators would act like competent and respectful leaders and not dictators, and staff could feel comfortable on the job and become vested in that company. But, unfortunately we are not living in an ideal world, we are existing in the real world where administrators abuse their authority and harass employees. The targets in these companies are usually those who are non-white. Yet, it is possible to establish a functional work atmosphere where these negative dynamics can be dissolved indefinitely. This will require a changing of the guards. In that, the autocratic dictator would be replaced with someone having a democratic leadership style. This is the type of leader who values the opinion of all staff and views each employee as a valuable member in the work environment. This leadership practice is ideal and produces productive outcomes for all community stakeholders. Moreover, this leadership style encourages and inspires staff members to contribute more to the work community. At the end of the day, there has to be better representation and support for Black employees within the workplace.

As Black Americans, living within an unjust society, if we neglect to take a stand, no one will do it for us. There is no such stance as, "United we stand and divided we fall." We have fallen two many times as a race for far too long, and we have yet to stand together in unity. This is not just about the adult Black male and female. It is about the livelihood and sanctity of our youth. Now we must make the change our Black boys and girls so desperately need to ensure that they will have a future. Being professional is not professional when others try to take away your livelihood just to feed their insecurities and hateful egos. As a race, we must remember that we are the few, the proud, the Black, and the brave. We are the guardians and directors of our own destiny. This is a truth we must be willing to embrace. We cannot allow others to control the trajectory of our professional careers. Otherwise, we will continue to be the underrepresented, underachieved, unappreciated, unsupported and unfulfilled in our pursuit of educational and economic equity. I don't know about you, but I am done with the foolishness. As a Black female professional, I give myself the charge of ensuring that young Black boys and girls have a future to aspire to moving forward in this current decade.

CHAPTER 6:
Homeownership and Investment Properties

When you mention the idea of homeownership or purchasing investment opportunities to the average American citizen, some people would express a sense of astonishment while others would cringe at the idea of having to deal with or manage such a financial undertaking with dread. There is usually a feeling of reverential admiration mixed with nervousness and dismay in addition to wonderment when considering the pros and cons of real estate investment. As potential homeowners, we are entitled and expected to have our reservations regarding the financial aspect of buying a home. In regards to becoming a property investor, we may also find that type of business venture even more risky. There are several questions which may arise at this point such as: do I have or make enough money to buy a home? You may even ask yourself, is my credit score high enough to reccive a home loan? As common and basic as these questions may appear the context of these types of inquiry are reasonable. Just the prospect of owning real estate is exciting for most people. Some families have gone decades without owning real estate. There are people who would rather rent than to own property claiming that the cost for upkeep is too expensive while others view the prospect of real estate investing as an impressive and productive move.

Despite your reservations, think about the potential in either becoming a homeowner or a property investor. For the most part, if you are looking to purchase a home do it while you are young enough to cut cost. This is a critical stage in your life where you can afford to make changes to your property and increase the value of your home. Some would say that investing in the real estate game is a benefit to the younger population. That statement is truer for young Black families who are often sometimes the first to become homeowners and investment property owners in their family. At this stage in your life, it is time to think about leaving a financial legacy behind for your children and their children. Sometimes we have to think about the long term goals by questioning, how can my financial decisions benefit my family in the decades to come? This thought may seem overwhelming in context, but believe me when I say; it is a necessary concept to think about. One thing I have realized in my lifetime is that my decisions are not just about me. Everything that I say and do in this world is a reflection of what I want to represent my family legacy. Never in my life did I want to become a product of my environment. I always wanted to become a change agent. That is why I myself became a Black homeowner.

Homeownership is a critical component of financial growth and economic equity. It plays a vital role in generating independent wealth. Furthermore, homeownership helps one to create and establish a stable home environment for the family, and it represents a form of personal growth and achievement. Homeownership also paves the way to financial freedom. However, today Black homeownership is as low as it was during the 1950s. According to Wake (2019), even after the 1968 Fair Housing Act, the U.S. Census data of 2017 showed that, "The percentage of U.S. Blacks who own their homes today is essentially the same as when housing discrimination was outlawed in 1968." With that in mind, homeownership for Blacks in America can be viewed as a double-edged sword. Although the idea of owning a home can be exciting, the challenges associated with that prospect can be more provoking.

For the average Black American this venture can produce either a favorable or an unfavorable outcome. The debt ratio for Black homeowners compared to non-Black or white homeowners is staggering to say the least. In addition, redlining and pocket listings are common practices which prevent Black Americans and other minorities from purchasing homes in certain neighborhoods. Some real estate brokers go as far as to maintain racially segregated neighborhoods. These are examples of how real estate brokers are still using unethical practices to reinforce racial segregation. In that, housing inequality is as unorthodox as any other social injustice Blacks are subjected to in this country. This is another issue robbing us of our rights as American citizens. We must speak up and bring about change in the housing market, so that all Black Americans can obtain homeownership.

In reality, whites do not face these challenges when they seek to purchase real estate properties. The experience for them is both trouble-free and uncomplicated. Therefore, whites do not view the process for procuring homeownership the same as Black Americans because they usually are able to purchase a home at a low percentage rate, are given a fair price, and are not being blackballed during the purchasing process. In the 1970s sitcom *"Good Times,"* the Evans family was the iconic Black household living in an impoverished Chicago housing project located in an impecunious community. Regardless of their many attempts to escape a life of destitution, the family never made it out of the ghetto. The family spent the remainder of their fictitious days living in a poverty-stricken neighborhood with no hope of becoming homeowners. For many Blacks, homeownership is like a "Dream Deferred." Similar to Langston Hughes' poem; therefore, the prospect of becoming a homeowner is a far reaching reality for some and a luxury and financial benefit for others, but for white Americans it has always been a privilege.

This raises the question, what does it mean to own your home? Well, in layman's terms homeownership means having a safe place to raise a family, living in an area which provides children with a good education, paying less taxes and saving more money, and having a peace of mind. Mostly, homeownership means built equity because it is the cornerstone of the American Dream. But in the eyes of many minorities, it has been another example of "The white man's privilege." For the Black American living in 21st century urban America, homeownership means freedom and financial security. It is one of our basic human and civil rights meaning the right to own property. In urban, suburban, and rural America, there are more Black renters than homeowners. This is due to a lack of education regarding homeownership. Some Black communities view owning a home as a financial burden instead of a financial benefit, not realizing that the former is a falsehood. This is what we call a paradox. The concept of a "paradox" refers to a conundrum or a contradiction in terms. In this case, while homeownership may seem unreachable to some, it is a real possibility for those who seek this privilege.

The Homeownership Paradox

Gone are the days of the fictitious narratives of Black lifestyles as depicted in 70s sitcoms like *"Good Times"* and *"Sanford and Son."* Those television shows did not represent Blacks as competent and successful human beings. Instead it was another form of mind manipulation which popularized, polarized, and glamorized Blacks residing in poverty-stricken neighborhoods as a norm. Moreover, the characters in those sitcoms were cast as the proverbial expectation for one being Black while living in America. As Black Americans, we reject those stereotypical false images. Those negative public perceptions of Blacks placed us in a metaphoric box. My interpretation is that the "American Dream" was never going to be a reality for those characters because they accepted what society deemed they were entitled to, and that was their downfall. Nonetheless, it is everyone's right to become a homeowner. Moreover, our approach to homeownership has changed drastically over the years. Now we have become homeowner connoisseurs who are well-versed in the housing market.

When it comes to homeownership you have to become savvy about your purchase. You have to also purchase within your tolerance. We should not purchase a $500,000 home just because we hit the 6 figure mark. Now, the approach is going to be different for each person, so let me give you a breakdown of the way I would do it if I could go back 15 years in my life. For a first time home buyer with parents that are broke and a household income ranging from $65,000 to $90,000, purchasing a home five times your annual salary rate is a foolish mistake. When I say parents that are broke, my point is you are not getting assistance or funding from any outside relatives or friends. In this case, you are on your own.

Therefore, the first thing you want to do is purchase a property at a discount. That would be a HUD home, or maybe a foreclosed home that you can add value with sweat equity, anything that can put you just a little ahead of the game with the salary you make. Next, please be prepared to sacrifice something, nothing great has ever been accomplished without great sacrifice. This is where you would have to figure out what you can tolerate. Do you want to decrease spending and put more on your house to pay it off in 5 to 7 years and maybe rent it out afterwards? Do you get a second job and continue to live how you live and just put the extra money on house payments? Or, do you stay in the house for 2 to 3 years, fix it up and rent it out? Renting it out will do two things. It will create an extra income for you, and it will allow someone else to contribute to your wealth building. The person or persons renting your home is actually paying your mortgage. Whoa! That's a win-win.

Your Dream Home

In regards to homeownership, the main questions asked are, how much can I afford, and what is your dream home? As a homeowner, you quickly realize that the benefits to becoming a homeowner outweigh the losses. Reflecting on the first question, you have to consider all of your expenses in order to determine what you can afford in reference to purchasing a home. You have to factor in any car payments and insurance you are currently paying, utilities, food and clothing. Usually, whatever is left over is how much of a home you can afford to purchase. Many people make the mistake of just considering the mortgage payment and ignoring the other monthly expenses. That would be a major mistake because that would lead to an immediate cascade of debt. Referring to question two, the answer is yes! It is important to think about your dream home. Buying a home is a tremendous step, so be certain that the home you purchase is the one you can see yourself living in for the next ten years or more. Homeownership is the cornerstone of the American Dream which solidifies that you have reached that pivotal educational and economic status in your life. Just remember that you have just obtained a piece of real estate. That means this is your estate or the property in which you own.

Another thing to consider when you are planning to purchase a home is the price. How much? That's right, how much? What is the purchase going to cost me? Am I going to benefit greatly from this venture, or will it completely exhaust me? Not just financially, but mentally, physically, and I guess emotionally for some. Many people are not up to this type of challenge, but for those who are risk takers, consider the following scenario. Let's take John for example; he is 25 years old and single. John's annual income is $100, 000, and he is looking to purchase real estate. Notice I did not say a home. John is a forward thinker; he has talked with mentors, real estate agents and read a number of books about obtaining wealth. John is definitely a real estate connoisseur. He has done his research, and now he is ready to purchase the property of his choice. John understands that owning real estate is a good long term investment. Furthermore, John knows that real estate is at the top of the list when it comes to obtaining wealth. When John first considered buying his investment property, his main objective was to generate consistent quarterly cash flow without the drawbacks. John's ultimate goal is to obtain independent wealth by purchasing real estate properties because he knows that real estate consistently increases in value over time and outperforms other investments.

Peace of Mind

Apparently, the road to homeownership varies for each individual, but the prospect of having "peace of mind" is universal for all homeowners. Buying a home can be as frightening of an experience as it can be a reward, but having a "peace of mind" makes the process more relaxing. No one wants to purchase a "house lemon." We want to make certain that our financial investment is greatly protected. We have worked too long and too hard to get to this monumental juncture in our lives, and we want to avoid any unnecessary expenses. Purchasing a home is expensive enough, we do not need to be worrying about the unexpected. That kind of stress would wear us down emotionally, mentally, and physically. Therefore, in order to avoid any type of undo stress I would urge everyone to purchase homeowners insurance for peace of mind. You can get insurance to cover the total rebuilding price for your home. You can even purchase insurance to cover any and all of your home appliances. Who wants to pay out of pocket for a new roof, or to rewire their home? That is the rationale behind purchasing homeowners insurance. Remember there is no one size-fits-all when it comes to homeowners insurance, so select the company and package that best fits your unique needs and the needs of your family.

This chapter places emphasis on the do's and don'ts of homeownership, so feel free to take advantage of these friendly suggestions before you make that final step of buying your new home. Keep in mind that this information is being presented by Black homeowners who want to see you blossom and obtain economic equity for you and your family. Homeownership is contagious. When your children witness your assertiveness to becoming a homeowner or a real estate owner, they are more inclined to replicate your success. It is all about developing your financial wealth and creating a legacy for your family as a member of the Black race. Homeownership is a category that most Black Americans have yet to venture into on their path to obtaining educational and economic equity. However, for every Black family who succeeds on this road, another Black family is sure to follow on this same path. This is how we as a race ensure that members of our communities see the value and benefit in owning a home or any piece of real estate. We want our brothers and sisters to understand that the idea of homeownership is about property ownership. Everyone wants to be able to say, "This is my home, or I own this property." That is the real reward.

Even in times of great despair like COVID 19, doing something unique and profitable for you and your family like purchasing real estate property is a plus. It is always a good idea to take your mind off of the madness and focus on something inspirational, and purchasing property to build that foundation is essential to financial growth. It does not matter if you graduated from high school, a technical school, college, or if you are a member of the armed forces, you have earned the right to become a homeowner. Let nothing get in your way. The notion is to gain equity. We all have our own convictions, ideas, theories and a suspicion regarding homeownership, but this is something we all should invest in as a race. Personally, I feel great dismay, and I am equally horrified when I read about so many Black families living in destitution while residing in poverty-stricken neighborhoods in deplorable housing. As a Black

American and as a human being, I want more for them. Everyone deserves to have a piece of the pie called the "American Dream" regardless of gender, race, creed, nationality, or their socioeconomic status in life. Property ownership is an ideal part of our civil democracy. As Americans, we are all entitled to that right as citizens of this country we call home.

Homeowner vs. Renter

Homeownership is an essential aspect to building up the Black community. It is a very necessary venture for the members in our communities. Let's face it, not everyone has the goal to become a wealthy businessman. There are so many things I wish I would have done at a younger age regarding property ownership. The examples given in the previous sections of this chapter were a reflection of the life choices I could have made at an earlier age to really put my portfolio in the millions. Although property ownership is not for everyone, I do realize that owning a home if you pay market value or below market value provides multiple advantages for not just the individual, but for our whole community. Homeowners keep an eye on their neighborhood; they form community watch and homeowner organizations. Homeowners take pride in their neighborhoods; they call police when they see suspicious activity. These are subtle examples, but they are very effective when it comes to keeping neighborhoods up. Just the opposite happens when you have a neighborhood full of renters, unless the neighborhood consists of high end renters. The average renter has nothing invested in the community and could care less about the activity in the neighborhood until it affects him or her personally. So, in short, the benefits of homeownership are more than financial. As we see our community as a whole, still in the same financial position we were in during the reconstruction period and no further ahead with homeownership compared to 1968 after the civil rights movement, we have to believe that there is some connection to the relationship of homeownership and progress in our communities.

Currently, there is a political and social debate focused on renters and homeowners. The premise of this debate addresses the social divisions between homeowners and renters regarding real estate property. For one, the attitudes and material interests between these two groups differ significantly. Renters are those who are tenants residing in another person's property whereas homeowners are those who own the said property. When we weigh the options of owning versus renting a property, we realize that homeownership provides privacy and is a good investment. On the other end of that spectrum, renting encompasses lower housing costs and short term commitment. The prospect of homeownership centers on more stable housing cost year after year, but the cost of renting a property increases excessively year after year. Even though there is no maintenance or repair cost for the renter, he or she does not experience pride of ownership and the tax benefits associated with building equity in the home. That is a reward reserved for the homeowner. When it comes to distinguishing between good and bad debt, paying rent is a monetary loss, but having a mortgage comes with low interest rates which make home buying affordable. After all, we will always need somewhere to live, so why not live in a home you own.

Basically, when we consider the financial impact of renting versus being a homeowner the benefits outweigh the circumstance. Unlike most other types of purchases, buying a home can be an extremely expensive purchase. We are talking about anywhere between the low five figures to the high hundred thousands for the average working class American. I am not speaking in regards to millionaires, but working class citizens who aspire to owning a home. The bottom line is that homeownership is the beacon of hope for the American family, especially the Black American family because it represents so many things. Homeownership means living in a safe environment, providing an efficient and quality education for your children, and obtaining financial security for yourself and your family. However, depending on where you live, your level of comfort may not be as high. But, if you live in a neighborhood that consists solely of renters, you will be taking a gamble. Some people find living in a renter driven community to be unsafe at times and disruptive. These types of living environments usually lack that sense of community and trust that you would notice in a homeowner neighborhood. For most families, safety is their number one priority when deciding on renting or buying a home.

Making the Right Purchasing Decision

Regardless of what you may have heard, you do not always have to purchase a home in the suburbs. Know that you have several options which lead one to question, how can I make the right decision when buying a house? Just remember that, it is okay if you want to buy a home in the city. In all sincerity, I understand why some people would hesitate in buying real estate in an urban area; I get it, but if you purchase the right property in the right neighborhood that value will always be there. So, we know that buying a home is an exciting adventure, and it is one of the most expensive financial ventures we will ever make in our lives. Even though buying a home can be a rewarding and profitable experience, it is not for everyone. Different people seem to make this decision at different stages in their lives depending on their finances. In this case, it is always sensible and proactive to consider your personal and financial goals at this point which lead to the following questions: do you want to have a monthly mortgage? Are you ready to place some personal items on the back burner for now? These are several questions you should consider before you invest your time, money, and effort into purchasing a home. Give yourself an opportunity to really digest that concept because home buying is a major step and an enormous responsibility that needs to be approached from multiple perspectives.

Consider the big picture by asking yourself; what are my long term and short term goals regarding this real estate purchase? Am I trying to create a lucrative business, do I want unlimited cash flow? Or, am I seeking to develop a sort of financial monopoly? We know that our reasons for purchasing real estate can be personal or strictly business. Either way, we have to be strategic while going through this process. First, we need to set some short and long term goals that are attainable to ensure that our investment objectives are met. The short term goals should be something we can reach within a matter of months like maximizing revenue. If you purchase several rental properties, you can lease the property for slightly more than the market value. You should also focus on reducing property expenses by getting the best insurance for the property and negotiating with maintenance companies regarding repair fees and materials. Knowing that real estate investments appreciate over time, it would be a good idea to consider practical long term goals such as keeping the real estate property in good condition in regards to upkeep. This can be accomplished by hiring a dependable and competent maintenance company. All and all, the overall focus is to earn an excellent investment return on your property and to keep the cash flow coming.

Regardless of your reasons for entering into a real estate venture, you need to make certain that you are fully aware that you need to make the right purchasing decisions if you expect to accumulate abundance in profit. Furthermore, you need to understand that this is not a decision that should be given little thought because this is a monumental step in your life that is both timely and costly. If you are not 100 percent sure that you should participate in the real estate game because you feel as though it is too risky, do not get involved in the venture. It is always important to know the risks before you get involved in anything that can impact your finances. Never do anything you do not feel comfortable with, and by all means always do your research. Read books, articles, watch webinars, learn about property taxes and property values, and attend conferences until you are educated enough to make the right decisions. Note that everyone has his or her own reasons for buying real estate. Some people buy real estate to own a lot of properties. There are those who purchase real estate properties to decorate and renovate to create their own visions like a duo-complex while others may invest in real estate to flip houses for a significant profit. Whatever your rationale, just make sure you make the right decision for you and your family.

Buy the Block

Buying real estate property requires you to have the monetary resources in addition to having sufficient to excellent credit to make the purchase. If your intent is to "Buy the Block" start off by avoiding making any frivolous purchases that may lower your credit rating and damage your credit standing. You want that FICO score to be in the high 700 range. Don't listen to anyone who claims that your credit score does not matter because it does. Your credit score tells the bank or lender whether or not you are credit trustworthy or a credit risk. Your goal is to be the former. Buying a block of real estate is not an easy task. In all honesty, it can be a very challenging and complex venture. With that being said, if there is potential in a specific neighborhood you are looking at excessive financial growth. But, if you purchase real estate property in a declining neighborhood, you can end up accumulating a massive financial loss. That is why it is always important to do your homework in regards to real estate purchasing. Never jump the gun. Make certain you are well-versed in all aspects of property analysis, the asking price for the property for sale, any financial or structure portfolios regarding the property, and conduct an inspection of the property and the area several times before making that final decision to buy. This reminds me of the 1986 movie *Money Pit* with Tom Hanks. It seemed like he had made a solid purchase for the property he acquired until the house and everything in it began to fall apart. It also relates to the "Buyer Beware Clause." Just note that it is wise to always be aware of what you are really getting yourself into before taking that final step to purchase a piece of real estate property.

Listen to your conscience and take heed to what is happening in the real estate market. The COVID 19 pandemic has created a lot of distress in the real estate market. Many people became unemployed meaning they did not have the monetary means to pay their rent or mortgage. This leaves the property owners to pay out of pocket for the rent and mortgages which creates a financial strain on their bank accounts. Instead of earning revenue for these properties, they are losing significant amounts of money. In turn, they may be willing to take on investors in order to maintain their properties. No one wants to profit from those experiencing hardship, but if this is a possible way to build financial wealth through real estate investments then do so. If not you, I am certain some corporate agency would take advantage of the situation. Just think of this as a major opportunity to buy property at a lower price in order to make a greater profit. With so many people working from home due to COVID, there are a lot of retail office spaces and restaurants that are struggling through this financial storm. Imagine being able to purchase a building that would usually cost the average buyer $500 per square foot for $250 per square foot. That is literally half the value and practically a steal. But, for someone like you or I, that would be the foundation for acquiring economic equity.

On the down side, you may want to avoid looking for cheap real estate purchases. Cheap is not always better, especially not in the current real estate market when things are so uncertain. During this critical time in history this pandemic has practically capsized the financial economy. There is so much possibility based on the tragedy of others. Basically, everyone's life has been upended in one way or another. It is difficult to discuss profiting from real estate investments in light of everything happening in the world, but sure enough life goes on and the economy has to continue to evolve as well.

In 1933 during his First Inaugural Address, President Franklin Delano Roosevelt made a candid statement regarding a depressed economy by saying, "The only thing we have to fear is fear itself." Those words resonate with me even today as I write about real estate pros and cons during this COVID 19 crisis. No one wants to buy property when lives are at stake, but the reality is that we cannot stop living because of this pandemic. As a community and as a race we must continue to move forward on our journey in life. Even if you do manage to purchase a property at a cheap price because of the current state of the American economy, keep in mind that quality will always supersede quantity.

As you sit there contemplating whether or not to "Buy the Block," or just a block of real estate in a specific area remember the old adage "You get what you pay for." So, think critically before you make that purchase. Do not be cheap, instead be wise. Know what you can and cannot afford. Try to be realistic about the purchase and not ridiculous. Over reaching your wallet and bank account is a major mistake some buyers often make. They place themselves in unnecessary debt because they overestimate what they can afford to buy in reference to real estate investment properties. Believe me when I say, owning a series of houses in a progressive neighborhood would benefit you as a property owner, and as a Black male or female trying to obtain financial wealth this would be a monopoly. You rarely hear about Black Americans becoming self-made millionaires from real estate ventures, but it does happen from time to time. Regardless if your aim is to purchase residential or commercial properties, know that you are building capital and creating financial wealth for you and your family. For every Black family that manages to obtain true wealth, another Black family has the same opportunity to replicate that process because each one can teach one.

Create a Monopoly

Equally important to the real estate game is the idea of creating a monopoly. You may be wondering, what is a monopoly? Well, a monopoly pertains to the exclusive possession or control of a commodity. In this case, the commodity is the product, object, thing, or piece of merchandise which holds a significant value being the real estate property in this scenario. This concept is similar to the board game "Monopoly" in which players participate in a simulated tournament involving trade and industry where players compete to rack up a series of real estate properties. Financial dealings and compromises take place to see which of the participants will end up controlling the majority of the properties and making the most profit. Like the board game, an authentic real estate monopoly consists of having a goal to purchase as many properties as one can afford. But, there are several underlining rules associated with this process which includes the buyer understanding the laws, regulations, and rules analogous to making logical and wise investment decisions. More than likely this will help you to invest in the most profitable properties. Needless to say, this can become a calculating process if you do not have an effective and well thought out action plan because strategy is everything.

When it comes to property investing, you definitely want to avoid making purchases that will not pay off in the long term. Always focus on your long term goals regarding real estate investments. Conduct a comparative analysis on various properties within the same zip code to check differences between sale pricings. Never allow yourself to become a "buyer beware victim." That is why you must always be persistent in doing your homework. Do not take anything for face value, and thoroughly inspect the real estate property you are planning on purchasing. If you represent yourself as an amateur, the seller will try to take advantage of your naiveté or lack of experience. A good buyer would consider the property value itself in addition to the potential revenue they can accumulate from renting the property monthly. Moreover, a good buyer thinks about the capital growth regarding the appreciation in value of the property stockpiles over a long period of time. Keep in mind that like the board game Monopoly, investment buying is inclusive of those same concepts. Therefore, no matter how much property you purchase or where you decide to establish your monopoly, you have to be well-educated and knowledgeable of the real estate market.

Even though this is the best time to really be pertinacious in your buying options when it comes to purchasing real estate. Think about the bottom line and the financial risks. It is very important to ascertain the differentials pertaining to taxes, penalties, and any other uncertainties which may emerge during the purchasing process. In other words, you must become your own critic. This is the time to be critical and evaluative in reference to your strategic planning. Making property investments is all about trial and error. The overall goal is to avoid as many inaccuracies and miscalculations as possible. Being a real estate owner does not mean that you have to do everything alone. If a difficult situation arises, it may be necessary for you, the buyer, to hire a professional. It is smart to have a second pair of eyes; someone who is well-informed about the real estate game. This pertains to someone who understands how to take action, has a clear vision regarding investment strategies, knows the facts about the real estate market, and has a strong grasp on the concept of property management. When in doubt, ask someone for help. However, if your intention is to go it alone just remember, be prepared for the unexpected.

Needless to say, the year 2020 and moving forward is the time to start making those financial moves. However, there are so many doubts and expectations surrounding the current real estate market in America. With the social unrest pertaining to police brutality of Black Americans, social injustices emerging in all avenues of life, and the COVID 19 pandemic, many people are finding themselves in the midst of great madness. With that being said, the housing market really seems risky to those seeking to purchase homes and businesses to increase their socioeconomic status in society. Even regular property investors are being cautious in their buying approach. According to *The National Association of Realtors* (2020), based on the global conditions of the real estate market, "With a low level of inventory of homes for sale and demand, the median sales price of existing homes sold has increased at a pace stronger than the increase in hourly wage growth since 2012" (p. 19). This leads current purchasers to become even more skeptical about purchasing real estate, but this is a matter of cost versus lost. When the cost is manageable, maybe the risk is manageable as well. However, if the risk is too high, it is definitely not worth the lost. It does not matter what type of finances you are dealing with, you should be practical and responsible in your decision making process because the choices you make can be damaging to your wallet and your livelihood.

The Main Real Estate Objectives

As we come to the conclusion of this chapter, there are several key points regarding our main purchasing objective that we all need to be cognizant of as potential homeowners and real estate investors which is to think critically, but to always make rational decisions. Our purchases should not only be profitable, those purchases should be meaningful and purposeful as well. You always want to set a clear market position. This is important to establish a strong constructive foundation on how to place yourself in an advantageous position when purchasing real estate. Be clear on your intent as a potential investor. Operating across the real estate property spectrum can be complex in nature. Make certain you have unique approaches towards residential and commercial property real estate. There are laws and bylaws associated with each entity. Corporate bylaws will explain the purpose for purchasing the real estate and the intent for the real estate investment, and the mechanics of the overall operation purposes of the business venture. Know that real estate law is based on state laws regulations regarding the purchasing of residential and commercial properties. Since federal law will be part of this equation, educate yourself on the Fair Housing Act for municipal purposes. You want to fully protect yourself while dealing with real estate transactions from a monetary standpoint. You never know if someone will try to manipulate or discriminate against you based on your race, color, sex, or nationality. It is a cutthroat world out there in the real estate business.

With regards to your main initiative for making the real estate purchase, start your journey by creating a list of potential properties that will bring in substantial annual revenue. There are multiple reasons why we need to consider engaging into the real estate market. One essential reason, regarding homeownership, would be to provide a stable, safe, beautiful, and loving home environment for our children, so they can become productive members of society by seeing how educational equity can lead to economic equity through hard work and perseverance. When we become homeowners, we are able to build equity in our homes rather than the money making a landlord richer and us poorer. As it applies to becoming a property investor, we can generate financial wealth through the appreciation of profit derived from the rental properties and commercial properties that we invest in to earn annual surplus. Know that the benefits of investing in real estate provide us with a stable cash flow and the financial leverage we need to sustain wealth. Moreover, the bottom line is that becoming a homeowner or a property investor can also yield excess returns for developing a type of diversification for a financial portfolio that can withstand the test of time. This is because our yearly gains regarding profit and returns are the ultimate monetary reward and an excellent reason for becoming a property investor.

In the long run, you need to ask yourself, what am I trying to leave behind for my family? Are you trying to accumulate great wealth, or do you want to leave behind a massive debt? These are questions we all need to ask ourselves on a daily basis because until we know the exact answer to these questions, we will remain lost, confused, and broke. Being a Black male or female living in America, we cannot afford to be naive in the world of real estate. For us as human beings, especially as Black Americans living in 2020, to have no knowledge or concept of the benefits associated with financial wealth and financial independence to change the trajectory of our lives would be a great tragedy. Remember, this is not about short term goals. This is a long term venture that will ultimately evolve into a legacy of knowledge, experience, and wealth. In reality, once we start our real estate journey we notice that along the way, once we begin to pay down our property mortgages, the cash flow begins to increase and materialize significantly over time; furthermore, paying down these mortgages does build up the equity in these properties. Even though the stock market fluctuates as well as the real estate market, be mindful that in all honesty real estate values often increase over the course of time. Therefore, a good real estate investment tends to create long term benefits to the owner. On a final note in this chapter, remember to be cautious and knowledgeable regarding any financial venture you decide to delve into, especially when it comes to what is best for you and your family.

CHAPTER 7:
Obtaining Financial Security

Obtaining financial security in America is more than a possibility, it is a necessity. Without financial resources, indemnity, and insurances regarding our own financial trusts, we are one step away from the poor house. Most Americans are living paycheck to paycheck without knowing when the bough may break. If this happens, a family can lose a large portion of their nest egg and possibly their home as well. That can be a frightening reality if we as Black Americans do not take our own banking and financial portfolios seriously. This can in effect become a detriment to the average American household, especially the Black family household since we are not safeguarded with "the white man's banking privileges and protections." In a nutshell, the goal is to avoid experiencing a financial free-fall. This refers to prices in the financial stock market dropping quickly and/or the economy plummeting significantly. This is based on the premise that the American economy is tied holistically to the Stock Market. When the market prices in stocks slump, our finances plunge, and if the market takes a serious dive, so will our wallets, financial portfolios, and our bank accounts.

Unfortunately, not everyone will obtain the financial security they desire in life to be able to provide for their families and have the financial resources they need to buy a home, purchase a car, make household repairs, travel, or to send their children to college. This is because of the financial and professional inequalities that exist in the American society. For instance, a school teacher is more likely to have financial security compared to someone working a 9 to 5 job earning minimum wage. People who work regular jobs are paid by the hour. If they show up for work and complete their scheduled hours, they get paid for those specific hours. However, if the same employees call out sick for the duration of a pay week, they will not receive a paycheck because they would not have accumulated time in hours to receive their pay whereas career jobs are based on annual salaries. If someone is absent from work, that person will receive his or her paycheck due to being a salaried employee. That constitutes as being a financial safeguard in the financial world regarding employment. This leads to money management where one effectively saves and allocates funds into various brokerage accounts to enhance one's financial resources in the future.

Past and Current Black Poverty in America

During the Great Depression, Blacks were the last hired and the first fired. Longevity in the workforce was a rare occurrence for Blacks living in America during that time period. A series of poverty stricken episodes in this country became a continuous cycle in the Black communities causing an economic downfall and financial crisis which devastated many Black families. The Stock Market Crash of 1929 caused a financial pandemic that crippled the housing market and halted the American workforce. Many Americans found themselves unemployed and destitute. This was especially devastating for the Black American. With the battle of racism already a constant in their lives now Blacks had to deal with the reality of being unemployed. From that point, many Blacks found themselves living in poverty. Lacking the financial resources needed to purchase a home or afford decent rent for acceptable living conditions, Blacks ended up residing in lower income housing. These houses or apartments were mainly located in the most deplorable areas imaginable.

But for the most part, economic inequality then and now has created a major deficit for millions of Black Americans due to systemic racism in the workforce, financial discrepancies regarding salary scales, and the lack of employment opportunities. Even today getting hired at local or fortune five hundred companies is a stretch for the average Black American regardless of his or her impressive educational and professional portfolio. These companies often see race first and skill ability never. I recall applying for this entry level job at a local company in the Baltimore metropolitan area. When they called me in for a face to face interview I was excited for the opportunity. When I spoke to the owner via email exchanges he seemed so overwhelmingly impressed with my schooling and work experience. I went to the local Macy's, purchased a two-piece Calvin Klein business suit and prepared for the interview. When the day of the interview came, I arrived at the interview site 5 or 10 minutes early. There were eight white males and three white females sitting in the lobby area who also applied for the same position. I will never forget when the white female manager entered the hall of the lobby and called me by name. When I stood up from the chair, her face turned pale, needless to say, it was downhill from there. I was not hired. I had the background experience and knowledge, but I had the wrong complexion for their company.

In reality, corporate America and the American financial banking institutions have never really cared about the financial well-being of the Black American. Our financial standing was never a consideration in the financial world. For them, we are a non-factor in their financial banking anomaly because of the false narratives they attach to our credit worthiness and our capabilities as human beings. Ironically, with all of our education, professional titles and positions in the world, we continue to bank white. Even though these racist institutions do not want to hire us, or demonstrate disdain when serving us, we continuously contribute to their growing wealth while our own aspirations to obtain financial wealth continue to be ignored and dismissed by these racist corporations. So I pose the question, when are we going to create our own banking institutions? Who is ready to step up and start supporting our community?

When Tyler Perry purchased 330 acres of land for $250 million dollars to build a major movie studio, he took a chance on his dream. He made his dream a reality by bringing it into fruition. If Tyler Perry has the insight and fortitude to manage his finances by making profitable investments, we all need to be bold enough to do the same. We do not have to be millionaires; we just need to be willing to trust our own judgment by investing in our own dreams.

The Financial History of the Black Race

Ideals of Black wealth have been shattered by social injustice and racial inequality for centuries. Through various attempts throughout the course of American history the Black man has ventured out to obtain financial wealth as a race to only be confronted with racial barriers. After the Civil War and the Reconstruction Era, Blacks were still at a major disadvantage in the United States. Despite the fact that Blacks fought for the Union during the Civil War and helped them win the battle against the Confederacy, once Blacks returned home they were treated as second class citizens and given no credit for their sacrifices in the war. Additionally, they had no companies and no land. Blacks were in the exact financial and social position they were in before the Civil War. The failure of the Reconstruction Period targeted Blacks by not providing a new era of reformed economic independence for former slaves or Free Blacks. This left them destitute; therefore, "Reconstruction ended as it began in violence and controversy" (Hine, Hine & Harrold, 2006, p. 445). However, shortly after the turn of the century we start to see Black neighborhoods emerging and beginning to thrive in areas like Tulsa, Oklahoma, Rosewood, Florida, and Winston, North Carolina.

Despite those marginal past successes, for many Black Americans living in current day America, the struggle continues. Blacks males and females are still facing social injustice, unfair treatment, and a lack of equitable opportunities in education, housing, and career advancement. These are elements which create poverty and financial unrest. Some people are enthralled with their current circumstance and refuse to take a chance on making permanent change in their lives due to the societal limitations and restrictions which continue to emerge in this nation which materialize out of hate. However, now is the time to start bringing about new change in a world consumed with so much loathing and divisiveness. It is the decisions and choices that each of us make that will dictate the future of this country and the trajectory of our individual lives moving forward. We cannot idly stand by and ignore the opportunities which are within our reach as American citizens. Instead, we have to embrace our potential to become even greater than our best selves. This journey is not just about you or me. This is a peregrination and a pilgrimage that involves an entire race of people. As the old adage goes, "Together we will stand, but divided we will fall."

When we reflect deeper on the financial history of the Black race, we begin to realize how far away from financial equality we really are compared to other races of people. This is not a trivial or baseless statement instead this is an unfortunate reality. Considering all the Black race has experienced in America, it is reasonable to understand why establishing financial wealth and security would be a benefit to our progress and our ability to position ourselves to get a fair piece of the philosophical American Pie. Let's face it, the United States of America has failed to provide Black Americans with fair and equitable opportunities to advance themselves both educationally and financially compared to their white counterparts. From a monetary perspective, Blacks are less likely to obtain financial wealth, especially when systemic racism and social injustice continues to be not only a barrier, but a major factor in this equation called life. James Baldwin once said that, "The brutality with which Negroes are treated in this country simply cannot be overstated, however unwillingly white men may be to heat it" (p. 326). Therefore, in order for the current financial history of Black Americans to evolve into a greater outcome and a plethora of wealth, our race has to acknowledge the sacrifices from the past and create a more productive outcome for the future of our people.

In reality, during the light of day, the decisions we make as a race impacts the success of our children and their children's children. Yet, year after year, and decade after decade, Black America continues to be subjected to the harsh mistreatment from an unfair and unjust America. It was once believed that to obtain the "American Dream" one only had to work hard and stay focused, now we know it requires so much more than traditional beliefs. It requires one having the fortitude to go beyond the binary expectations in life. Unfortunately, for the Black race, we are still a nation within a nation. We will never be one nation under God until racism is dissolved in this country once and for all. The financial history of the Black race is immersed in the seeds of radicalism, extremism, and systemic racism. As the years continue forward the concepts of wealth and inequality continue to broaden even more exponentially within our society. According to Bricker, Henriques, Krimmel and Sabelhaus, "The preferred concept of wealth includes all assets over which a family has a legal claim that can be used to finance its present and future consumption" (p. 266). However, in conjunction with the economic inequalities which exist currently in the United States, this ideal may not seem realistic in the eyes of the average citizen, especially not the average Black American due to the financial constraints he or she may currently be experiencing in society.

Seeking Financial Security

What is the actual prospect of financial security in American society? Are we truly able to reach the goal which stems so greatly from the American Dream, or are we merely deluding ourselves with such fantasies that are beyond our reach, especially as Black Americans living in an unjust society. For us, perhaps the reality of obtaining financial security is just a dream, or is it a dream within a dream. I don't know about you, but I prefer being debt free. Being in debt to me is a life sentence. I appreciate my freedom. Who wants to owe company money for the rest of their lives? That is definitely no way to live. Even though seeking financial freedom can seem like a an overwhelming task, the benefits outweigh the time you have to put into the process. You have to think about this undertaking as building a financial legacy for you and your family. The goal is to gain long-term control over your family finances. But, before you begin this financial venture, you need to have a starting point and a set amount to save and invest. You also need to conduct a thorough evaluation of your current financial status. Are you pleased with your financial situation, or do you believe you need to make a change? Then proceed by grasping the true meaning of financial security.

In a world where financial security is a fundamental aspect regarding productivity outcomes for monetary profit, we tend to pose the question, what is financial security? Is it having millions in the bank? Is it having a high paying job? Is it having a set of skills that are marketable? I'm not sure any one of these alone gives someone financial security, but the combination of these attributes creates a barrier around the investments of a household. It is my opinion that to have a stable financial portfolio in today's society, you have to have multiple streams of income. You also need to become truly educated about the mechanics of money, and know how taxes really affect your overall cash flow. Additionally, you need to have the motivation and drive to produce something that we would call financial security. Think about how many millionaires filed for bankruptcy, or how the 2008 crash depleted Americans 401k and forced some that were prepared to retire to work for another 10 years. If those examples do not make you pause and consider the urgency in obtaining financial security for you and your family, I don't know what else will make you take this matter seriously.

As I look back at my high school years, I think about the hell I gave my mom about not wanting to attend this accounting class. What she didn't know is that I was skipping class to hang out in the hallways. As an adolescent I had no idea how this class could help me in life. The class was very boring, and it did not have any relation to the world I knew. Let me say first, my parents did a remarkable job raising four children in a poverty stricken, crime infested neighborhood, but when it comes to managing money they did not have the education to properly prepare us for financial success and security. What they did teach us is how to create multiple streams of income, to never depend solely on one job or one way to make money. In retrospect, I realize what a true benefit that class could have been for me. Imagine if I would have learned to read financial sheets and knew the value of calculating assets and liabilities before making purchases, big or small. Wow! Can you imagine how secure my financial portfolio would be today? I can, 1 million, 2 million, 10 million.

Get the Money

So how do we create this so-called security? Capital, capital, capital. That's right you have to "paper" in this world, but capital is much more than the legal tender we use to buy groceries and clothing. Capital is real estate, stocks, patents and copyrights. Anything you own or possess that can produce more is what capital is. It allows a person or business entity to compound their efforts by continuing to replicate the use of its product. There are many ways to have your money make money, or your capital to produce more capital. The most reputable and well-known financial guru or advisor would say, "Buy real estate or stock." Moreover, they would tell you to invest in a profitable business. These are good choices, but how does a person that lives paycheck to paycheck invest in stock, or invest in real estate, most of us can barely put enough money together to save for a rainy day. This is why we must decide what is most important regarding our financial success. Do we continue to buy trivial items we do not really need, or do we make a profitable investment? Remember, where there is a will, there is always a way to the well of prosperity. Anything is possible in life. You just have to believe enough in yourself and take a chance. Too often I hear people complaining about what they don't have, but they refuse to invest in themselves enough to breathe life into their dreams.

For many of us, especially Black Americans, this idea of "getting the money" seems like a distant dream. But like any dream, obtaining financial security can become a reality for the Black family. We all understand that individual circumstances and economic conditions can impede our goals and act as a contributing factor in preventing us from obtaining financial wealth, but we must look beyond the scope of reality in order to locate our "golden nest egg." Please understand that, I am not a tax advisor, a legal advisor, or a financial planner. I am just an American citizen sharing my own experiences. So, if you feel as though you do not know how to proceed with obtaining financial security on your own seek the advice of counsel. From an objective perspective, I would say do your research and make realistic choices, but trust your judgment. For strictly informative purposes, I decided to discuss the need to build financial security to those who may not have considered the possibilities available to them for changing the trajectory of their current financial situation.

Basically, get the money you need to start with, and stop procrastinating. You cannot afford to temporize, stall, delay, or hesitate any longer because time is running out. You are not getting any younger, and your family needs a win. Say to yourself, "Today is the day I change my financial destiny." Don't live by the world's rules! Live by your own rules! If you want to survive financially beyond the confines of living from paycheck to paycheck be diligent in your strategic approach to your financial planning. The world is your oyster. Knowing that the United States of America has the highest per capita income compared to other world countries is a comfort when considering one's financial options in the housing and banking industry in addition to the stock market. For me, I have a mortgage and I love traveling the world. These luxuries cost money, and I know that in order to make money you have to save, invest, or start a business to bring in more revenue. So, if I aspire to become independently wealthy, or to travel the world extensively, I need to change the dynamics of my financial situation.

Banking While Black

The phrase "Banking While Black" may sound somewhat odd to the average person, but for the Black American we know this concept all too well. The probability of receiving effective banking advice from racist financial institutions like Wells Fargo, Citibank, and Chase are slim to none. These banking institutions are like vultures waiting to catch you at your weakest point, so that they can start to feed off of you. Wells Fargo executives have been poaching off of Black Americans since the dawn of time. In the article entitled *The Racialized Costs of Banking,* Faber and Friedline (2018) assert how, "Balance requirements are higher and fee structures are more punishing among banks in Black and Latino communities net of controls for socioeconomic characteristics and the presence of competing financial services" (p. 7). Even though one of the aforementioned institutions claims to be "learning from the past and transforming for the future," that is not what has been going on with either of these banking agencies. For decades, these financial institutions have been charged with predatory lending practices and policies, and a bunch of other immoral financial exercises that lead to the deterioration of cities across America. Of course the largest portions of those cities were located in urban areas.

Our main objective regarding the banking aspect of our lives is to be treated with fairness, dignity, and respect from these obviously racist financial banking establishments. But, how can Black Americans obtain financial wealth when the odds are against us? What are we supposed to do when we are denied loans and lines of credit we qualify for based on our impressive salaries and good credit ratings? Economic equity is but a dream deferred when one's rights are being violated by corporate banking conglomerates like Wells Fargo, Citibank, and Chase. The average citizen does not have a chance going up against a multimillion dollar corporation unless he or she has the financial capital to withstand their corporate reign. Historic and present day racial practices among banking institutions is such a common practice that some people are not even aware that they are being discriminated against because of the color of their skin. As a consequence, not educating yourself about the financial market can set you and your family up for a financial free-fall. The goal is to avoid a financial crisis. "During the Great Recession, comparably-sized banks closed at higher rates in markets serving communities of color between 2009 and 2014" (Faber & Friedline, 2018, p. 8). This created a financial domino effect for Blacks who banked with Wells Fargo, Citibank, and Chase by causing them to lose their bank accounts and owe thousands of dollars in banking fees.

In addition to inequalities in income and in wealth, Black Americans have to deal with racism in the banking system. This is another avenue of the social injustice we are subjected to as a race. Yet, regardless of the financial disparities that exist in our country we need to strive to achieve financial security to protect our families from financial devastation. There is a saying in the financial world, "risk versus reward." In that, as consumers, we need to focus more on the financial reward and less on the risk. Banking while Black is not a catch phrase, it is a reality because when Black Americans deal with banking institutions in this country they pay higher fees for everything from bank accounts, credit cards, and mortgage loans. Banking institutions provide people of color with the least amount of credit by charging them the highest rates. This is the type of social injustice and inequality Black Americans have been subjected to for decades. If and when our financial circumstances improve, it will only change by our actions, and not by the actions of our oppressors.

A Prescription for Good Financial Health

With a financial forecast ahead pinpointing the economic downfall in the American economy no one is actually certain about what their financial outlook for the future will be this year or the next, but we still need to find a remedy for our financial ills. Our finances need a cure and now. This is definitely a matter of urgency for Black communities and the Black race in general. There are so many white billionaires like Jeff Bezos, Larry Ellison, Bill Gates, David Koch, and Michael Bloomberg in addition to many others in America that it puzzles me why our race is so destitute, especially since we live in one of the richest countries in the world. But, as a woman and especially as a Black American, I know our financial situation is mostly due to the injustices we face at every level of the social and economic hierarchy in this country. Out of the 705 billionaires in the United States of America, 76 percent of those billionaires are white. That number speaks volumes about the inequitable, discriminatory, unjust, preferential, and partisan world in which we live. Even though this is unconscionable, it is a reality. These statistics are both alarming and extremely troubling to me as a Black American. Furthermore, this is confirmation that there must be a financial paradigm shift in this economy, so that Blacks can benefit from the capital gain on the financial hierarchy as well.

Despite the financial challenges that lie ahead, Black Americans still have to maintain the idea of financial prosperity. A prescription for creating good financial health will be based on our ability as a race to change the financial paradigm to benefit our families in the near future; if not in 2020, then hopefully within the next few years. Keep in mind that the United States continues to have the highest per capita income compared to other countries. The prosperity of America has always been based on its economic progression and yearly growth. Although distribution of goods and services have an impressive history in our country, the distribution of wealth among its citizens has not been as profitable, especially since Blacks are recognized as one of the poorest racial groups in America. For example, a 2019 study found that over 97% of respondents vastly underestimated the huge gap between the median wealth held by Black families ($17,000) and White families ($171,000)—a ratio of 10 to one. These are some disturbing numbers that represent income inequalities in America between Black and White Americans. There is a mask of deeply repressed inequalities which regulate the financial positions of Blacks in this country. Politicians and government officials alike have the ability to manipulate our financial status and keep us oppressed within the financial market unless we as a race change the script regarding our financial situation.

For the average Black male or female, the prescription for achieving good financial health comes with a price, and involves plenty of hard work, diligence, and commitment. Let's face it, the economic state of Black America is staggering because there is such a significant absence of Black wealth in America. While Black Americans continue to experience poor economic conditions, their white counterparts continue to prosper significantly. Compared to white Americans Black Americans are barely surviving financially. However, in an effort to shift our current financial situation, we need to make smart and profitable investments and purchase more property. Real estate has always been the most practical and safest option for investment. Real estate guru Warren Buffett is a testament to this reality. Unfortunately, immoral and unjust policies limit access to minorities when it comes to obtaining capital wealth. This especially holds true for marginalized groups. For Black Americans seeking profit in the financial world, real estate is the best option for acquiring economic wealth besides becoming instantly rich and famous by luck. But, as long as economic disparities continue to exist in this country, the probability of Black Americans reaching financial wealth at a growing rate will be next to impossible. For now, the first step is to clear up your credit history so you can purchase real estate and create your own financial monopoly.

Know Your Rights as a Consumer

Moving forward in the pursuit of accomplishing financial security, Black families need to be well-versed regarding consumer rights. Under state and federal law everyone is entitled to the legal protections pertaining to consumer rights. The information listed on your credit file should always be accurate and up to date. Unfortunately, that is not always the case. When we find ourselves in a situation where we are being treated unfairly and unjust, we have a right to dispute the information in our credit file. Essentially, your credit file is what determines your creditworthiness. If there is information on your consumer report that is false, fraudulent, misleading, or antiquated, you have the right to have the statements removed. You do not have to accept any false narratives that place a negative mark on your credit record. This is another form of social injustice that keeps the Black American from prospering in life. For decades, credit agencies would let these statements linger on the credit reports of Black Americans intentionally for years without any regard for the sanctity of their creditworthiness. These were fraudulent attempts to keep the Black male and female oppressed by rejecting their right to obtain lines of credit to purchase a car, pay for college tuition, or buy real estate property. As surreal as this may sound, this is a reality even today in some cases. The main question is, what are we as a race going to do to change this dynamic?

Although this can be a delicate and time consuming process, it is indeed a necessary act that must be achieved to confirm and obtain financial stability for the Black family. I say the Black family because we do not have "the white man's privilege" in any avenue in society. As a people, we work hard for what we get in life. We earn our education, excel in our careers, buy our ideal car, and purchase the home of our dreams through sheer old fashion work ethic, dedication, and persistence. Nothing is given to the Black race; we produce the fruits of our own labor just like we produced the fruits of the American economy during the period of slavery. As it relates to our rights as consumers, we must be steadfast in our attempts to clear our credit record by contacting the credit bureaus: Equifax, Trans union, and Experian. It is even more important to remember that Experian is the credit bureau that controls the FICO score, so be mindful of that number especially because it carries the most weight on your credit report. Moreover, be diligent in your efforts to improve your credit scores and keep those numbers above 700 points. Always remember there is an obvious difference between a want and a need. A want is a personal desire or luxury, but a need is essential for one's survival, and we all need to have good credit.

No matter what your dreams and aspirations are for your financial goals, make something happen that will benefit both you and your family. Know that the statute of limitations is on your side. Creditors must remove negative narratives from your credit report by the end of the seventh year. However, any bankruptcy information can stain your financial record for as long as 10 years. That is why it is so urgent that people pay bills on time, and stop making unnecessary purchases. The money you use to purchase something you "want" can go towards paying off your debt. It is essential that Black Americans think strategically when it comes to their finances. Check your credit report once or twice a year minimum, and check yourself as well. Avoid making unnecessary purchases that can bring down your credit score. We already know that the Black American credit score number starts at zero whereas the white man's credit score starts at 500 points, but that is a story for another time. Just pay cash whenever possible, and avoid using your credit card for impromptu purchases. If you do not have the cash to pay off that credit purchase within 25 days of the billing cycle, do not use plastic. Instead, use the paper money. Once you obtain your credit report start restoring your finances back to health.

Restoring Your Financial Health

Yes, you can control your finances! Everyone is in a position to obtain good financial health, but it requires a lot of work. The initial stage deals with improving your credit score and keeping it above a 720 FICO score. If you have old accounts that are damaging your financial status by lowering your credit rating, you need to pay those accounts off in full. If not, creditors will label you as a risk and avoid doing business with you. Therefore, paying your bills on time within the 25 day billing cycle is a necessity. Be a responsible consumer by paying your bills on time each month. The reality is that you never want to carry over debt from one month to another. However, if you happen to carry over debt from month to month try to eliminate that debt within 6 months or less, and know the difference between a want and a need. You may want to make a small or large purchase, but the question is, do you want to place that purchase on your credit report? The relevance of having a good to exceptional credit score is something they do not emphasize in grade school. This is a lesson you often learn from life experiences through the process of trial and error.

Another step on the road to controlling your finances and improving your credit standing deals with you understanding the concept of money management. It is more important to save than to spend. If you spend your money foolishly, you will end up in financial debt. You need money to save money. Having no money means not being able to save for a down payment on a house, or having a full purchase payment for a new car. Lack of saving money also means that you will not be able to travel locally or abroad on vacation, or enjoy the finer things in life. Instead, you will just be living paycheck to paycheck never having any money to do other things. Money management refers to having the ability and monetary means to save, budget, invest, and monitor your spending habits. Everyone should create their own financial portfolio to keep track of their saving and spending. To just wing your finances would be ill-advised at this juncture in your life. Prepare for the future by repairing your financial health. Never put off for another day what you need to do now.

Remember that your financial health improves your physical health as well because you find yourself less stressed when you have full control over your finances, and that provides you with the "peace of mind" you need when building your financial wealth. Additionally, being mentally and physically healthy improves your mindset and keeps you focused on the task at hand. You should approach your financial goals with a clear understanding of purpose, and with a realistic perspective. With that in mind, you feel much happier with your life because you know you have banking safeguards in place. Since everyone has dreams and aspirations to own something in life like a home or a business, it is imperative that you are mindful of the financial decisions you make which can either impede or advance your financial health. This is not just a reflection of you as an individual. It is a reflection of us as a race because too many Black Americans find themselves in some sort of financial limbo. But, once we gain control of our spending habits we become more productive, and we begin to notice that we no longer have issues making our monthly mortgage or car payments, and there is plenty of money to save, and use for family vacations. Eventually, all of your hard work will pay off in the end, especially once your credit history has been restored to good health.

Contemplating Your Financial Future

There is a no holds bar approach to securing one's financial future in spite of the barriers which one may encounter along the financial path in life. Regardless of the obstacles we may encounter at every turn along the road, we must remember that our purpose is to attain and promote economic empowerment for ourselves and for our families. Achieving educational and economic equity is the cornerstone to the philosophical American Dream. With that goal comes great sacrifice and dedication. Nothing in life is easy, and if it was going to be easy, it would not be worth it. Making the decision to invest in your future and that of your family should always be your main focus in this world. People like Warren Buffett, Bill Gates, Bernard Arnault, Jeff Bezos, Steve Ballmer, and Mark Zuckerberg have made millions by investing in their dreams. Sometimes it just takes having a purpose and a vision and being objective about establishing your own greatness. Just knowing that the financial position we take in life provides us with some sort of illumination or incite into various possibilities life has to offer. With opportunity comes great reward. Wealthy white men who own and operate private institutions in America did not take their opportunities likely instead they took advantage of those moments and profited greatly.

Basically, one must keep in mind that every situation demands a different set of strategies. Our financial future is contingent upon our willingness to become accustomed with paradigm shifts in the financial market and in the banking system. When our economy is growing we witness an increase in the national income, but a contracting economy is an example of a declining economic trend. Economic fluctuations in the American financial system can have a domino effect on even the average citizen trying to build a financial reserve for his or her family. Therefore, in order to create financial wealth and establish economic growth, Americans, especially Black Americans need to commit to changing with the times. As asserted by **Bricker, Henriques, Krimmel and Sabelhaus,** "Some distributional shifts in income might be attributable to fundamental economic factors such as skill-biased technological change, but this probably does not explain increased income concentration within the top 1 percent" (p. 268). While considering the emerging trends in the job market and those in the banking institutions, we know that accessibility and drastic generational shifts in the workforce have altered economic outcomes for Black Americans in this country.

Consequently, not everyone knows the best path to take on their financial journey, especially when there only exist faint prophecies of equality in this nation due to excessive racism, social injustice, and the ongoing dismissal that "Black Lives Matter." Unfortunately, remnants of inequality continue to plague this nation as politicians continue to spin negativity and promote race divisions in America. Yet, for every single person living in this county, there is an undying truth that each of us has the ability to succeed academically, professionally, and financially regardless of our current circumstance. We must continue to believe that behind every door is a room filled with possibilities because within this world, the loss of hope of making any kind of monetary wealth can become a frightening event in one's life. This is because the lack of money can limit the mobility of the Black man and woman. For Black Americans, this type of financial constraint can either make or break us, or leave our families in a financial slump. That type of turbulence is something that can destroy a generation and disrupt the future trajectory of a race of people.

CHAPTER 8:
Benefits to Social Networking

Social networking is the premise for establishing strong professional and personal relationships with people who can help us expand both professionally and financially. Just like your environment has an impact on your development, the same applies to the company you keep. You have to have a good team surrounding you. With that being said, the people around you should be those of a like mind. They should have a good idea of where they are going and it should be similar to where you want to be. Now, do not confuse that with being courted by "yes men." You need people around you who will challenge your ideas, but still support you. Even if you have some who are not 100% committed to your goals, their help is still important. As intelligent human beings, we have to recognize that with the proper leadership, multitudes of small contributions are what create grand achievements. Just imagine how many committed day to day workers it took to build the Empire State Building. Now, think about all the not so important people who only showed up once in a while to deliver material, or to deliver tools. They didn't need to commit fully to the task, but their contributions were still highly impactful.

When we relate those concepts to present day America, we consider the multitude of relationships it takes to build a productive and influential social networking system. This process requires creating a sort of populated list of influential people who can help us catapult our social and economic standing in life. The intent behind this endeavor stems from a business perspective instead of a personal perspective. These are relationships that branch off into the social, financial, professional and political realms of society. From there we can establish reputable relationships with other professionals based on individual and mutual needs and beliefs. Building a strong networking base is essential to establishing economic equity. Even during the age of the Empire of Mali, many people forged relationships to compete for political and economic power. However, we are not talking about ruling the world, but creating a comfortable and productive economic outcome for ourselves and our families. To be able to create such a networking system demands vast communication with other individuals with similar social, political, and financial aspirations.

Rightfully so, it takes a strong network to bring about positive change and productivity outcomes for an individual and particularly for a race of people in general. Being a Black American, it is essential for me to build a strong networking system for developing effective and purposeful professional networking relationships in addition to establishing financial growth outcomes that will benefit me and my family for decades to come. It's all about creating a legacy and establishing generational wealth for our family and their families after them as we look towards the future in our decision making process. Therefore, if my intent is to create a family or community of competent and productive individuals during my lifetime, I know that I have to be committed to the task. Although this is indeed an exhaustive exercise, pressing forward to accomplish each of these social, professional, political, and financial goals, it is imperative to remain constant on this economic journey. Communication is the key to building an effective and affluent social network. In retrospect, when I reflect on the network of educators I have bonded with throughout the course of my professional career, I have come to realize just how beneficial and profitable those relationships have become to my current position as an educator. At this juncture in my professional journey, I am well-versed in curriculum and pedagogy. I am a true change agent within the educational field, and I am a master of my craft. People learn from other people. We need those relationships to steer the course of our lives socially, professionally, and financially because with wisdom comes educational and economic equity.

Who's Ready to Ride?

If you believe you are ready to plunge into social networking to improve your social, political, professional, and economic standing in life, then start driving and take that long ride down the road of network building. Let's think about networking for a minute. Oprah Winfrey networked with Bill Cosby, thus becoming a self-made billionaire. Tyler Perry networked with Oprah Winfrey in turn he became a multimillionaire. I could go on and on, but you get the gist. It is not always what you know in life that propels your social and financial standing, but who you know in life who can send you on the path to success. These days nothing is easy. Since the integration of technology, building those personal and professional relationships in the world have become exceedingly challenging to say the least. Tyler Perry and Oprah Winfrey each have over a million followers on Instagram and other social media platforms, so the probability of me meeting either one of them is slim to none. Therefore, I need a contingency plan for expanding my social network on a realistic platform to get the attention of those I plan to network with both inside and outside of my immediate networking circle.

From a social perspective, networking involves building relationships that can benefit and propel your social status. Right now, you may be wondering, what do creating social relationships have to do with becoming more productive in life? Well, to put it simply, it has everything to do with it. You can be the smartest and most unique individual in the world, but if you do not establish relationships with other people who can help you advance in life, you are sabotaging your own future. As the saying goes, "It is not what you know, but who you know that makes a difference in this world." This reminds me of the first time when I wanted to get out of the classroom and take on a leadership position. Since I did not know the administrators that well and I was new to the school, I did not receive the position. Once I started building a strong network with my administrative team they started to give me more responsibility. I started conducting professional development workshops on and off site. Then, the following year, the principal made me an Instructional Support Teacher also known as an IST. Just imagine what the outcome would have been for me had I not been intelligent and assertive enough to build that social network with my supervisors and colleagues. Taking action always leads to obtaining true and profitable results.

On another note, it is important to understand that political relationships can help build those financial relationships you may need if you intend on purchasing real estate, opening a business, or running for some form of political office at the state or local level. This process relates to networking with the so-called "political movers and shakers." These are people who have political clout. Can you imagine building lifelong relationships with a group of influential people with political power and leverage? You could possibly rewrite your entire narrative. In current day society, people of authority continue to dominate the political and the economic market. It does not matter if you are a liberal, a democrat, or a republican, the goal is to create a networking system that can withstand the test of time. This is how we as Americans and especially as Black Americans obtain financial sustainability in such a corrupt economy.

While dealing with the inequalities of the social structure in which we live, we as Black Americans fully understand that the Black race has always been the most oppressed minority group in American history. That statement alone should convince us as a race to press forward in our pursuit to obtain both educational and economic equity if we have any hope of changing the current oppressed narrative associated with our race. We are and have always been a capable, competent, and creative race. Now is the time to change the social, political, professional, and financial dynamics for our future generations of young people. We must change the direction of our current plight in the United States of America in order to truly feel like a citizen of this so-called great land.

In reference to professional networking, we build these relationships for career advancement because it is difficult to excel professionally in an isolated bubble. Anyone who aspires to achieve professional progression in a specific career field must be willing to bridge the gap and sometimes mend relationships within the workforce environment. This requires an overhaul of restorative practices that promote internal productivity outcomes for members at every level of the work community. There are three fundamental ways to disintegrate the professional bubble, so you can gain access to constructing your own tower of connections as an employee, but you have to be ready to ride out the process. You must first expand your horizons by exposing yourself to new ideas, evolving your thinking process, and executing more effective work methods. Additionally, you should consider making a dramatic and impactful change in your professional status. Last, you must understand that as professionals, we adapt and grow through a series of regulatory changes; therefore, in order to morph into an accomplished professional butterfly, you need to create your own networking bubble, and negate those antiquated notions about goal setting that use to apply to career advancement.

As we reflect on building economic equity for ourselves and our family, we tend to establish a connection with a group of people who can help us bring our ideas and aspirations into fruition. Everything we do in our professional careers should be geared towards attaining professional achievement, economic equity, and financial empowerment. The very essence of networking breeds stability. Practically every man, woman, and child in this country understands the concept of becoming someone of greatness even beyond his or her wildest dreams. It is those expectations of self which motivate and inspire us to excel in this world. Imagine how wonderful it would be to advance significantly in a professional career or in the financial market. Orchestrating such a strategic plan requires determination and commitment. Considering how Tyler Perry managed to network with Oprah Winfrey was a tactical move on his part because Oprah has the financial standing, and an impressive networking clientele. Becoming friends with someone as financially and politically established as Winfrey opened many doors for Perry. This is relative to the idea that, "It is not what you know, but who you know." Having friends in high places is always a plus, but having friends in low places will only leave you in the dust living a dark and limited existence.

Remember when you got your first car and everybody hung out with you, you became the most beloved person in your crew, and overnight you started to pick up new friends. If you were going to an event, you did not have to look far to find someone to ride with you. Now time has passed and your car is no longer in good shape, you are starting to miss events and coming to gatherings late because of your car problems. You might have to push your car a few blocks a week to get it out of traffic so that your uncle Charlie can work on it later. You began to see who is really committed to the ride or if someone is just looking for a ride. This is kind of the same process for determining who will be a part of your social network. People you can depend on in times of hardship and in times of triumph. You want to surround yourself with those who motivate, inspire, excel, and strive for success. Those are the ones committed to riding with you on that professional journey. Individual competency is attributed to the support one receives from his or her social and professional network which confirms the end result. Reflecting back on the car scenario, it is important to note that people who are there from the beginning of your journey in life will more than likely be the same ones in your corner towards the end.

The Absence of Networking in the Black Community

It is both staggering and surprising to realize how the lack or absence of social networking drives Black unemployment. Not being a partied to the same social network system as other cultures and races makes it difficult for the Black male and female adult to advance significantly in the workforce. It does not matter how many college or university degrees you hold or your impressive GPA because it has never been about what you know, but rather who you know. The lack of access to credible and substantial networking resources can break a career and stagnant one's productivity on the job in a specific career field. When we consider the lack of networking within the Black community, we begin to realize how disadvantaged the majority of Black Americans are in the working community compared to their white counterparts. In this instance, there is no evidence of equitable outcomes when the disadvantaged are not given equal access in the work community because of the lack or absence of networking opportunities available to them. Basically, the Black American is receiving the short end of the "philosophical employment stick." This continues to be a reality for the average Black person who resides and works in America. Even though this is the year 2020, unemployment continues to rise in the Black community, and career opportunities continue to deplete for the Black race.

This chapter addresses why networking is essential for Black Americans to obtain economic equity in America, and how this country's race division and greed continue to disrupt the very possibility of making the American Dream for Blacks a tangible reality. The actuality is that, in this particular country, a nation dominated by one race makes it difficult for other races to obtain a piece of the American pie. This creates a massive "racial wealth gap" in the economic system. The poor get poorer, and the rich continue to get richer. The idea of obtaining economic wealth is a crucial part of our personal and professional goals from elementary school to adulthood. With financial wealth, we are able to leave behind a prosperous financial legacy for our families. Establishing generational wealth provides the average American with the monetary resources he or she needs to sustain financially in the world, but if you are unemployed there is no legacy to leave to your family and their family after them in the long run. Instead, there is only destitution and broken dreams. It is greatly the hostility, disunity, division, and estrangement of the American people that makes equality a far reaching reality for Black Americans.

The purpose of chapter 8 of this book is to provide the American people and especially Black Americans with suggestions as to how to obtain economic equity for themselves and their families. It has always been a misconception that Blacks do not aspire to advance themselves in life. Confusing as it may seem for some people reading these pages, the fact is that Black Americans have been disenfranchised by the United States government for so many centuries that Black Americans have become immune to the repetitive and unjust treatment their own country has forced upon them since the dawn of time. As a nation, the United States of America is not only a country divided, it is a nation in agony. Until Black Americans are afforded the same professional and financial opportunities as whites in this country, there will always be a massive race division in America. However, as a race, Black Americans must take matters into their own hands by creating a social networking system within their own immediate sector that is far-reaching and more prevalent than any other social network that currently exists in this world. That is how we create our own economic destiny and change the current financial trajectory for Black Americans for the better.

Exploring the concept of networking within the Black community is the premise of this chapter because without establishing an effective career networking system, we will not be in a situation to excel as career professionals. Instead, we will continue to perpetuate a continued cycle of oppression in a country that not only despises the color of our skin, but our very existence as a race in general. Having a steady well-paying job provides financial stability; it builds the family unit, and establishes a level of success in one's life. These are the very fibers that thread us together as a race. Therefore, it is imperative to know that the absence of effective networking systems within the Black community will only suppress us further from advancing in society on both a social and economic level. James Baldwin said it best, when he stated that, "… the spoils of injustice, anarchy, discontent, and hatred are all around us" (p. 63). Therefore, we can no longer afford to continue to be concerned about white America because white America is not concerned about us.

Strategies for Building Effective Networking Relationships

History has proven that there are a series of effective strategies to build lifelong and effective networking systems to improve the socioeconomic status for Black Americans in this country. If those networking policies, procedures, and practices have been effective and efficient for the white population, those same tactics would be beneficial to Black America as well. Recently, there has been an unprecedented public outcry in the Black community to ensure that Black Americans receive the financial opportunities they deserve to open small businesses, purchase homes, make lifelong investments, and send their children to college.

Most recently, that profound voice has come from Ice Cube who was born O'Shea Jackson, and he has publicly announced that the social injustice in this country has to cease, and he has demanded that the United States government develop a financial contract with Black America. Ice Cube is using his celebrity platform in a productive and selfless manner to gain national support in his political initiative to improve the economic trajectory of Black urban communities in America that are immersed in poverty and limited in opportunity. All of this stems from the aftermath of the Black Lives Matter Movement in response to the recent race killings of Breonna Taylor, Ahmaud Arbery, and George Floyd.

As a result of this aftermath, many people in America are beginning to speak out against racial injustice and demand a call to action from the American government who dictate policy and enforce laws. The policies and practices of the Civil War period do not coincide with the current state of the world. This is the time to change the economic imbalance in this country and to ensure that Black Americans receive the entitlements which have been due to them since the dawn of time even before your parents and mine. This all refers back to the lack or absence of networking opportunities in the Black community because without allies and supporters there is neither advancement nor opportunity to grow and prosper. Having a limited education and job opportunities means having a limited life due to lack of resources. As a public school teacher, I have a front seat on seeing how a Black community ravaged in poverty-stricken surroundings and raised unemployment struggles to survive from day to day, and how uneducated people living in these communities end up selling drugs, using drugs, or killing each other for sport to obtain some sort of financial gain. Unfortunately, unless there is a major paradigm shift in how Black Americans are living in these urban communities, they will not be able to branch out and develop effective networking relationships with other communities and agencies that can change the dynamics of their living situations.

Reflecting back in time, from the reign of the first Black King of Africa, Mansa Musa, to the most memorable and beautiful Black African Queen of all time, Queen Nefertiti, the Black race has always been known for our accomplishments and strengths in the world. Yet, we live in a society in which our heritage of royalty and significance continues to be ignored. However, to ensure that Black Americans continue to become the race of Kings and Queens as depicted in history before the days of slavery, a series of effective networking strategies must be put in place to help Black America advance on the worldwide stage in education, politics, and in both the financial and housing market. Networking strategies that assist Black Americans in raising their living standards such as establishing economic equity which promote the following:

- Workforce full employment strategies
- Equal pay for equal work strategies
- Strategies to improve education in urban cities in America
- Protections on voting rights for Black Americans in this country
- Strategies to improve the injustice which exist in the criminal justice system in this country

Overall, these political based networking strategies will be beneficial to the average Black person residing in America in such an immersive and profound way by helping them to become more productive in a country that limits their productivity levels because of race or ethnicity. These strategies refer to improving education and employment opportunities for the Black American in this so called "Land of Opportunity." While these are several key strategies that need to be implemented and acted upon, nothing will change the current economic state of the Black American in this country if we continue to remain silent.

Unfortunate but true, if we are to see any element of educational and economic growth for Black American citizens in this country, significant change has to happen. Therefore, in order to improve the socioeconomic outcomes for our race group, we must instill within our own communities a renewed sense of pride, unity, and purpose. These are unprecedented times in our nation and within this global economy. From a stereotypical perspective, when politicians and the average layman speak on the unfortunate circumstances of the Black American, they are basically reflecting on life in the inner-city. However, we have Black Americans residing in urban, suburban, and rural areas in this country who are equally suffering financially due to the lack of equality in this country. Injustice and inequality are not isolated in one micro system. When it comes to networking in this country, the micro system one is born in can either hinder or advance someone's educational and professional career just based on the immediate relationships established within the community alone. Needless to say, the people we surround ourselves with have an impact on our economic and professional standing in this world which ultimately initiates our future financial wealth or lack thereof.

Gain the Upper-hand

Within the United States of America, the white upper class has the monopoly on financial, social, and professional networking. In order to build an affluent networking system, Black Americans have to network like "A rich white man." This involves developing a strategic plan to capitalize on the A-listers in society. We are not living in a one for all, and all for one society. In the year 2020, more than ever, we find ourselves living in a capitalistic America. The rich progress and the poor get eaten or devoured like cattle. Considering the actions of the current presidential administration that is an accurate assessment. For the past four years, Trump has been vocal on disrupting the core of the American fiber. He has incited the actions of white supremacists, denounced racism in this country, and refused to make a peaceful transition of political power to the incoming presidential administration. All of Trump's rhetoric has woven a thicker blanket of racism in our country, and made it even more stressing and difficult for Black Americans to develop an effective networking system to help us propel out of the financial slump we find ourselves in today in 2020. It is now up to the American people to band together and create change in this unjust political system which continues to isolate and mistreat the very people whose ancestors built this country.

In both my personal and professional opinion, it is never impossible to change one's economic position in this world. All one actually needs is opportunity and will. The networking connection is based on who you know in the professional and financial world in addition to who knows you. When you ask yourself, who knows me? You may respond by thinking about your parents, partner, spouse, close friends, and immediate family members. Regardless of how much love and support you may receive from your immediate base of people, they are not the ones with the networking connections you would often need to excel in a professional career or to increase your finances unless they are educators, established and successful business owners, or they work in the banking and financial industry. Too often people make the mistake of obtaining advice from people who are not qualified to provide a realistic and effective response because they are not experts in the position in which you seek. The lesson here is to remain steadfast and to be cognizant that in the pursuit of equity in this country mindfulness is essential regarding networking. Moreover, remember that it is essential to connect with the "Movers and Shakers in this world." In the end, who one knows and what the people he or she knows is willing to do to support or guide them on their educational, professional, and financial journey in life is the major imperative in this scenario.

Since the beginning of time, mankind has delved deep within him or herself to discover who he or she is in this world. While some people may argue that self identity is acquired independently, others may argue that who we become personally, professionally, and financially in life is a process which involves a collection of many people, experiences, and adversities we have encountered in this world as individuals. In the book *Baldwin: Collected Essays,"* Baldwin writes, "All of the Western nations have been caught in a lie, the lie of their pretended humanism; this means that their history has no moral justification, and that the west has no moral authority" (p. 404). Having experienced racism myself being a Black female growing up in the mid 80s as a youth, I can relate to the experiences which Baldwin found himself as a young Black man of the 1930s and 1950s while living in America. Like then, the experiences Black people encounter and are subjected to in America today continue to be solely based on race differences. America still has not wrapped her head around the fact that this country is a melting pot, and that each of the elements in that pot create a unique flavor that is essential to creating a great meal. With that being said, how can America be great if she refuses to be merciful? Even in the year 2020, this country refuses to embrace each of her children and provide each of them with equal protection under the law and equal opportunity in education and employment.

In order to gain the upper-hand in this world in regards to improving one's academic, professional, and financial status in life requires diligence, commitment, and assertiveness. As a Black man or woman living in America nothing is given to you for free. You have to work hard for what you want out of life. I mentioned this before in the book that there is no such thing as "Black privilege in America." On the other hand, Black hardship is a reality for our race in this country, and we need to come together as a group to change the financial dynamics of Black America for the better. This is not an individual pursuit, but it is a collective act to decrease levels of unemployment for Black Americans by providing them with jobs that provide a living wage. It is a promise to young Black boys and girls that when they grow up they will be afforded many opportunities to live a comfortable life free of poverty and financial hardship. For too long in this country, Black America has not joined forces to shift the financial status of our people. Instead, we just accepted the 1% wealth that white America threw at our feet by allowing an extremely small percentage of the Black race to participate in the movie industry, the music arena, the political system, and in the financial sector on Wall Street. Keeping this in mind, we as a people must create effective networking relationships in each of the aforementioned business arenas if we are to gain the upper hand in this current financial world.

Networking as a Person of Color

When has networking ever been fair and accessible to people of color? Even in the year 2020, Black Americans find themselves blackballed from being privy to professional and financial networking systems that whites have had access to for the majority of their lives. Major corporations like Amazon, Google, and Microsoft employ little to no Blacks in their organizations, especially not in the corporate departments of these professional institutions. Despite the obvious, this is an unequal and unprecedented phenomenon which has overshadowed the capabilities and opportunities for Black Americans since the beginning of American history. Career advancement opportunities that are available to white Americans are not available to Black Americans because the concept of "networking" is different for people of color compared to their white counterparts. As a Black woman in America, networking to obtain professional advancement is a challenging endeavor. In reality, I have less of a chance of becoming a college professor at a prestigious university with a professional degree than a white woman with no degree. For some people, the color of their skin opens doors quickly while it takes years and sometimes decades for the rest of us to reach progression in our professional lives. Even today this is an unfortunate constant which exists in the professional world in this country.

In spite of the pandemic our country has experienced this year, America continues to be divided in reference to race. Therefore, networking to get ahead in life as a person of color has become even more complicated and complex in this harsh social climate. To get ahead, Black Americans need to expand their knowledge of professional industry in all equitable systems. We cannot allow ourselves to be limited in knowledge and skill ability. With networking comes leverage, and we need leverage to even out the balance in the American economy which benefits the average Black

American who is currently living in less than desirable conditions. Believe it or not, there is always opportunity where there exists possibility, and in this world anything is possible.

Since we have had a Black president and a Black first lady in the White House, and now we have the first Black female Vice President of the United States of America, I am willing to believe once more in the American Dream. The late Reverend, Dr. Martin Luther King said it best when he spoke against unjust laws and unjust law enforcers when he stated that, "We refuse to believe that the bank of justice is bankrupt"(p. 138). Over the course of decades, Dr. King forged relationships with political leaders in America like John F. Kennedy and Robert F. Kennedy to bridge the walls of racial divide before his assassination on April 4, 1968 in Memphis, Tennessee. He used his social and political networking platforms to bring people together in discourse. It is by reflecting on his words and actions that we march forward to create our own networking system.

A recent question I find myself pondering is, how much more can the Black race handle living in an unfair society where we are not afforded the same rights and privileges as white Americans? Do we accept what this country deems fair for us, or do we make changes for ourselves as a race? As unfair and unjust as this country has been towards Black Americans, I refuse to place my future and the future of my children, and my children's children in the hands of the American government and political leaders that run this nation. This is supposed to be the "United States of America," but there is more division than unity emerging from this land. To this day the networking industry continues to be at the forefront of this capitalistic society we live in as citizens of a divided nation. As an American citizen, I recognize that our only recourse is to determine the next steps in becoming participants and winners of the networking game within a society divided by race. This is a reality that must be acknowledged by each Black American residing in America. Each year, this country seems to drift further apart which weakens the economy and threatens the moral fiber of the principles this country claims to base its religious and legal practices upon. This places Black America in a financial deadlock, and limits our educational and economic future. Therefore, establishing a strong networking system is essential to achieving one's academic and economic goals.

With risk comes reward, and with hard work comes change, but the right connections can make life easier and your goals more attainable. Regardless of your current socioeconomic standing, you have to see the relevance in creating a viable social network system with the right people base. The purpose for establishing a professional network is to increase your productivity outcome as a professional, an entrepreneur, or as someone just seeking economic advancement. Since the inception of COVID 19, career opportunities have become scarcer in this country. The idea that creating a networking system can provide career opportunities to the unemployed, provide the necessary resources one needs to enhance his or her skill-base, establish long lasting relationships between political allies, and bridge the gap between the rich and the disenfranchised. When you find yourself and your family between a rock and a hard place, you will do everything within your power to remove those obstacles out of your path. This is the point in your life where you decide whether or not you want to be identified and labeled as "A Have" or "A Have Not." It is all about taking risks and making logical and profitable decisions.

The fundamental principles associated with establishing an effective and efficient social base of influential people derives from one's ability to create a functional system with consistent financial benefits. If success is what you want, you have to dedicate the time and effort to build and maintain those equitable relationships you will need to get ahead in life. Furthermore, you must maintain those relationships by recognizing the common threads in which you can identify the political and social beliefs and practices that you share with a particular person, company, or agency. Consider this to be your professional hemisphere. In order to become the best of the best, you need to immerse yourself with people who are positive and successful change agents. Associating yourself with inspirational and motivational people will challenge you to excel in your professional career while helping you increase your financial status. In order to propel forward in this world on a higher economic stage, we need to be challenged to take the risk. But, to truly understand the concept of professional networking requires building relationships with a variety of people who are in leadership positions and have the financial, political, and business connections that can help you advance in the corporate and financial market. This involves the following actions:

- Developing a profile of "A-list" contacts
- Attending conferences and popular networking events
- Participating in informational interviews to expand your brand and network with other companies
- Establish long lasting relationships with influential people to build the leverage you need for future endeavors

Historically, from the 1970s through the 1990s, it was common practice to have face to face meetings with business and Hollywood executives and corporate bankers if you were the average person trying to get ahead in life, but those opportunities are now nonexistent in current day America due to COVID-19. Now everything is about social media and who you know in order to get a leg up. This is an unfortunate reality for the average professional or layperson. Basically, creating a profitable social networking system is contingent upon one's ability to understand the concept of capitalism. When the United States of American was founded in the late 1700s, it was constructed on a capitalistic and economic system where private individuals and businesses own capital goods. Under this economic system there has always been a disproportionate distribution of wealth in American society. With that, the rich get richer and the poor remain poor. This is a major disadvantage for the average American, especially for the Black American who is already the victim of an unequal and unjust society. However, in order to change the dynamics of the economic realities for Blacks in America, there has to be equal access to financial banking institutions to create small businesses and to rebuild Black communities, especially those located in urban areas. After all, fairness creates opportunity.

As we begin to focus on the necessity of the networking institution, we begin to understand the urgency in developing a list of influential "A-listers" or clientele who are the most respected, well-known, and established people in various segments of society. It doesn't matter if it is the sports world, film and television, the public and private financial sector, or politics, it is always imperative to have friends, associates, and allies in high places. It is mainly about constructing relationship capital. Despite if you have long term or short term goals, it is imperative to ask yourself a series of viable questions such as, what is my purpose for building a networking system? What are the rewards versus the risks? Where do I begin to establish these relationships, and how do I go about initiating these tasks? Although finding the answers to these questions will be challenging, it is not an impossible endeavor. For the average person taking on such a challenging undertaking may seem virtually impossible, but it can be accomplished as long as you are willing to apply yourself. Just remember to never take anything personal. This is purely business and your approach to the networking process should always be professional.

CHAPTER 9:
A New Beginning

Even though the American Civil War ended on May 13th, 1865, the remnants of that war continue to haunt Black Americans to this day. The end of the war meant that Black Americans were free people. They were sent on their way to establish a life for themselves as American citizens, but like most things, freedom was not free. One hundred and fifty-five years later, race continues to be the most damaging, destructive, and devastating horror in American history. But, as Black Americans we say, "This is the year of change for our race!" Now is the time for the new beginning we have aspired to accomplish all of those centuries ago in this country. The hypocrisy of the theme, "The Land of the Free, and the Home of the Brave" especially when Black Americans are not free to excel educationally, professionally, and economically in the nation in which they were born, and in a land in which their forefathers and foremothers helped to establish through blood, sweat, tears, continuous financial struggle, and many wrongful deaths at the hands of white supremacists and racist cops.

Ironically, we are currently waiting for the results of the 2020 Presidential Election to determine whether or not the political aspect of change will take place in an already divided nation. Either we will bridge the gaps of diversity, or we will end up shattering the very foundation of this country to its very core, and we cannot afford another Civil War. Instead of losing life, we need to focus on enriching and extending the lives of the American people, especially the lives of Black Americans in this country. Historically, when Blacks mention the unfairness of this country, they are accused of "Playing the Race Card." There is no single race card. In all reality, there is a "Race Deck" because the odds of obtaining the greatest heights of educational productivity and financial and economic advancement have always been stacked against us as a race of people. To this day it astounds me how so many other racial groups continue to ignore the academic, social, and financial injustice Blacks have tolerated or been forcibly subjected to for centuries.

This leads one to wonder, is it me causing these oppressive outcomes and actions I have experienced as a Black American, or is it the unfairness of the country in which I was born? Just the idea of knowing that if you are born Black, you have no privileges in America even though you are a natural born citizen of this country is perplexing. Strange as it may seem that is a daily reality for Black Americans. Some days it seems as though we are foreigners in our own country. Can you imagine walking in a department store and the first thing someone says to you before giving you a friendly greeting, and most of the time the friendly greeting never comes, is what are you looking for? All of this is happening the moment your black face walks across the threshold to the store. Multiply that experience by 100, that is how often I have experienced that type of situation repeatedly in my lifetime as a Black female. The first thing people see when they see a Black person is race. You could be a doctor, a lawyer, a mother, a business owner, or a wealthy individual, but if you are Black trust and believe your blackness supersedes your professional and economic status. Now, imagine being Black and uneducated, and not having the financial or economic resources or stability in life. That situation and those strange occurrences become even more unbearable.

However, regardless of the situation one finds him or herself in life, what some people view as the end, can in all actuality be the beginning of a new life story. In retrospect, when I consider that I was one of eight children, I know that I was blessed to advance in life. This is not an isolated possibility only given to the few. It is a reality that is afforded to all who believe in themselves and know that they deserve better in this world. I am a firm believer that every American and specifically every Black American has the ability to alter and change the direction of his or her life. Opportunity is for every man, woman, and child regardless of skin color or race. Therefore, never allow a country to dictate to you what your future will be. Take your future in your own hands and mold your life into fruition. In that, the two essential questions we must ask ourselves are, do we remain content in our current state of reality, or do we take the initiative and strive for something better for ourselves and for our families moving forward? If you believe in new beginnings, take a leap of faith and change the current economic dynamic of your educational and financial circumstance by getting more educated and increasing your financial worth. Keep in mind that as Americans, we always have the potential and opportunity to start anew because this country does have the assets we need to excel at all levels in life.

Changing the Direction of Our Future

Strategy is everything when seeking change. The course of action in which we take as Black Americans will determine the outcome of our lives. Knowing that we have so many students graduating on a fifth grade and lower level by the time they reach twelfth grade is disturbing. This is a systemic issue that needs to be addressed on a local and national level. How can we expect to change the economic status of our race if our younger generation of citizens are not educated enough to sustain themselves in the workforce, or have the intellectual ability to create and establish new businesses that can funnel money and resources back into the Black communities? It all starts with the family unit as mentioned earlier in chapter one of this book. Family is and will always be the epitome of change. The change can be positive or it can be negative change. If the aim is to ensure that every Black boy and girl in American society has an opportunity to succeed in this world, the family unit needs to be mended for the betterment of the child. I am not saying that mothers and fathers who are not together have to get married, but I am saying that regardless if the father lives in or outside of the home, he needs to contribute to the child's future financially, socially, and spiritually by providing unlimited support for the child. Children advance greatly when they receive love and encouragement from both of their parents.

Knowing what we can do together as a race to change the current state of our educational and financial affairs in this country is unlimited. There is no limited number of things we need to address because our resolve demands constant and repeated dialogue and action. True change agents bring about the trajectory of a given situation or event. They do not stand idly by and make baseless comments and hopeless suggestions. Instead, a change agent takes immediate action that makes a greater impact on the lives of many people, and not just their own life. As a child I knew that I wanted to obtain the "American Dream." That was my main focus as a youth. I understood the value of a college education, having a career paying job, having transportation to get around, and the importance of homeownership. Since I was intelligent and wise enough to consider those ideals in life as a Black child living in America, I am certain that the children today aspire for those same things and much more. What is it going to take for us as a race to realize that something has to change with us in order to bring about change for the younger generation of Black Americans? Children are innocent beings. They never asked to be born in a world consumed with such hate and indifference. They only want to be able to live.

Going through the motions is not enough at this point. How do we expect our Black youths to be able to sustain themselves in an American economy that has been structured against them from the very beginning if we do not bring forth change in the education system, in the banking system, in the political system, and in the housing system? Systemic change is the nemesis against systemic racism. Moreover, it is our collective actions as a group that will provide our current and future generations of Black youths with a better socioeconomic future. For far too long Black America has been buying into the false promises of political leaders, especially the spin and rhetoric of presidential candidates who have mesmerized us with glamorous campaign jargon. Unfortunately, it has taken several decades for us as a race to realize that it isn't about selecting a republican or a democratic candidate as President of the United States of America. The true purpose for giving our vote must be for the purpose of electing the candidate who has our best interest at heart, and who lives up to his or her political promises. Currently, it is now 12:26 pm on Tuesday, November 3, 2020, like most Americans, I am awaiting the results of this political farce to see who will be the president for the next four years, and whether or not that president elect does the job for the American people, especially the promises made to the Black voter.

Taking the initiative to vote for a presidential candidate who you believe will direct this country on the best and right path by enhancing our economy to help rebuild the lives of many Americans is a universal goal for most voters. Our financial, economic, spiritual, and physical health has never been in greater peril as it is currently in the year 2020. With COVID- 19 still a reality, unemployment high, and a country divided, we are witnessing America in turmoil. Not since the Great Depression has our country faced such massive uncertainty. The scale of destruction the next four years can cause the Black American if the wrong presidential candidate is elected is a frightening thought, but I firmly believe in the good citizens of this great country. When I consider the protests against social injustice, police brutality, and unfair treatment of Blacks that white Americans have been attending, leading, and supporting over the past four years in this country, I feel even more proud to be an American. Their actions showed me that regardless of our differences there is much more that makes us the same. We are all Americans regardless of our race or creed, and we should always think of ourselves as being "One Nation under God." As Americans, when we decide to choose the path of righteousness our entire country and its entire people will have an opportunity to succeed; this will create a visible path of hope instead of a trail of hopelessness.

Refusing to Accept Handouts

If someone were to tell me that accepting handouts was an act of oppression, I would ask them why? However, I am intelligent enough to face the hard facts. After all, when it comes to manipulating the American people into giving up their vote, providing political handouts is a key factor in this equation. Winning is part of the "American Way," and using underhanded tactics to guarantee that a political candidate wins a presidential election is no different from trying to win The World Series or a Super bowl Championship. The players are aggressive and assertive in their actions and execution, and the crowd watches in the bleachers. Those of us sitting in the nosebleed seats have less of an advantage to see what is actually happening before our eyes while those located in preferential seating have the greater benefit in this political arena. They receive the political favor while the less advantaged receive the political falsehoods. Even in 2020 this type of masquerade continues in the American political system. The rich get richer and the poor get poorer. Receiving handouts is the equivalent of receiving nothing in the political world because politicians give you weightless words to serve their political agenda. Once the election ends, they usually go back to their party's agenda and negate the promises they made to the American people, especially the promises they made to the Black American voter.

In all reality, oppression is what has always held Blacks back in America. The American presidency has been at the forefront of oppression in this country. The President of the United States (POTUS) is the dictator and ruler of the people. His words dictate the direction and actions of the American people as a whole, or as separated pockets in society. At 1:26 pm on Tuesday, November 3, 2020, I am counting down to the last hours of this chilly afternoon awaiting political results that will either support The Black Lives Matter Movement and Black Americans in general, or this election will start a race war. People have been calling and texting me all day warning me about the possible violent aftermath and carnage that may emerge from the 2020 presidential election. I have to admit, just receiving those calls was troubling to me as a Black woman living in America. I began to question my own safety; will it be safe for me to travel to the local Wal-Mart for food, or to have dinner at a local restaurant? Will this election be a new beginning, or the beginning of the end for Black Americans in this country? Regardless of the outcome, I have already decided to refuse to accept political handouts and to vote for and support the presidential candidate I believe will help to bring about economic change for the Black race.

These presidential candidates need to realize that instead of giving us a handout, they need to provide us with a hand up. We would like to move up the ranks in the military, in the professional field, in the business world, in the financial system, and in the political arena. Former President John F. Kennedy's inaugural address reads, "Ask not what your country can do for you, and ask what you can do for your country?" His words alluded to the ideals of human survival, individual success, and freedom for all men and women. But, when a race of people are not afforded great opportunity and treated unjustly within the country in which they were born and live, how can they make significant progress? Kennedy's words represented and inspired hope for the progression of all people regardless of race or creed; however, in current day America, even the words of President John F. Kennedy, have fallen on deaf ears. In a country divided, contributions Blacks make and have made to the nation are often ignored or disregarded as to have had no value. Even now, no one in politics these days are actually listening to the cries of the people, nor do they care about the needs of the people, especially the needs of the Black Americans living in this country because America continues to be "The White Man's World."

If the "white man" is given opportunities to obtain riches, the Black man should be afforded those same opportunities and advantages, but in my lifetime that has yet to happen. There are basic principles in life that we all must adhere to as a country, but some races of people appear more principled than others, especially in an unequal and unjust socioeconomic system. I wish that race wasn't an issue in this country, and that people would be given opportunities based on their knowledge and character. Yet, that is not the case in the world in which we are currently living. In present day American society, we have to take risks on electing the right people for the right reasons. I am not going to vote for someone because they are black, white, male, female, rich, or poor. My vote goes to the person intent on bringing about substantial, effective, efficient, significant, and impactful positive and productive change to a country drowning in racism and smoother in hate. Before I advance myself further in this country, I have to be able to walk freely in this world, and not be concerned with being denied opportunity based on the color of my skin or the texture of my hair. Yes, I am a Black person who lives in America, but most relevant is that I am a Black American who happens to be a natural born citizen of this nation.

When to Know Enough is Enough

For the duration of my lifetime, I have heard white politicians make false claims about how they intend to help the Black people and the urban communities in this country. If I am an adult of 50 years, what does that tell you about the country in which we live? What it tells me is that nothing has really changed. Cities build housing projects. Landlords raise rent so high that no one can afford to pay. The landlords in turn sell the land to the city when they cannot get anyone to live in their high rental properties. Then, the city takes the land and builds more projects or low income housing. This becomes a repetitive cycle, and minorities get stuck living in lower class neighborhoods where prospects of homeownership is nearly impossible. In the early 1970s and late 1980s, deteriorating global economic conditions set off a catastrophic ripple effect in the American economy. Similar to the effects of The Great Depression, America found itself poorly prepared again for a financial crisis. With this country facing a questionable presidential election, unemployment high, economic growth on the decline, and racial tensions escalating, it is difficult to say what tomorrow may bring for the future of every American, but I can say without a doubt that the socioeconomic conditions for the average Black American will change for the better in the very near future.

At this point, we should be saying, "Enough is Enough!" Although we exist during these questionable and disturbing times, there is hope for change. If change is not given to us by the educators, politicians, bankers, and housing institutions, we will establish our own schools, banks, housing institutions, and elect Black politicians who are committed to improving the economic conditions of urban communities and the people who live in those neighborhoods. For every 50 year block in American history, the Black race finds themselves in the same conundrum. The idea that every half of a century no substantial economic progress has been afforded to Black Americans is disheartening. It is evident that now the actual change we seek as Americans has to come from within our own racial borders. We cannot afford to depend on the weightless words of politicians and government officials. Campaigns are generated by political parties to communicate persuasive dialogue to intrigue and sway the American voter. However, in 2020, the average voter has heard these songs and slogans enough to know that those statements are nothing but rhetoric. The past days of manipulating the Black voter and getting a free ticket into the White House is over. Now we expect something in return for our vote. This year we are looking for economic equity and financial advancement.

As an educated-professional, a homeowner, a mother, and a successful Black woman, I know when enough is enough. If opportunity is stripped from the hands of one group and placed in the hands of another, that is not equality. Black people want to see a repudiation of the direction for this country. The 2020 Presidential election confirms there exists a cultural divisiveness that ignores Black victims and supports oppression. The political views right-wing Americans have regarding their personal and financial entitlements are mind-blowing. American history alone is consumed with racism, slavery, redemption, white supremacy, and segregation. For citizens of a country to continue to support racist groups and a racist president, demolishes the very moral fiber and code of the United States Constitution that speaks to the contradiction for preserving freedom and justice for all. Additionally, forging political relationships with people who support white supremacy and engage in brutal acts against a group of people is both immoral and unconscionable.

By acknowledging the racial barriers which exist and divide this country, there is an immediate urgency for Americans in support of the Black Lives Matter Movement, and those who value all human life to join forces with Black Americans in the pursuit to create an America based on peace, love, respect, and harmony because hate only poisons and destroys a country. Hate leaves no room for productivity, progress, or positive change instead it corrupts the mind, body, and soul. As a child, I promised myself that no one and nothing would stop me from succeeding in this world. I also promised myself that I would always protect my family by any means necessary. Those words hold true for me even today in the year 2020. When I reflect on my personal motto in life, I attribute my wisdom to my faith in God at such a young age which has always given me hope. I believe that if a person does not believe in something greater than him or herself that person could fall for anything and accept anything. Looking at the 2020 presidential election those words have never been truer. At this current juncture in time, we all should be saying, enough is enough! This current election has proven that Black lives are so transactional in American politics. It appears that Black lives do not matter to governors and senators, and that we may possibly have to endure another four years of this current presidency.

Decisions worth Fighting For

Even though the right to vote is a civic and fundamental privilege for all Americans, there are those who refuse to exercise their right to elect government officials. This can negatively impact election results because each vote does count. Unfortunately, during the 2020 presidential election shifts in public opinion and race relations have altered the wholesome ideals of most American citizens. Race issues and the massive protests which took place between 2019 and 2020 either promoted or discouraged those undecided citizens to cast their vote for this current election. Reflecting on the 2016 Presidential election, we noticed how several red states turned blue while more blue states turned red like Pennsylvania. However, in 2020, Black Americans understand that having the freedom and ability to make decisions for their future, the future of their family, and the future of one's race is a huge undertaking to say the least, but it is indeed a necessary endeavor. That is why most Black people voted in local and general elections in 2020 to support the political candidate who has their best interest at heart. The thought of people ignoring their own voice and refusing to vote because they do not agree with or like either candidate is absurd. In this world there are antagonists and protagonists. Either you vote for the potential hero of the people, or you elect the devious and dangerous villain. It is either one or the other.

Difficult as these decisions may be, there will always be choices one has to make regardless of personal beliefs and possible risks because life matters, and especially Black Lives Matter when we reflect on how many Black lives were senselessly taken in this world. Thinking about Black people who were lynched and murdered for being non-white in America and daring to voice their ideas makes me cringe to the very core of my bones. Emmett Till, a 14-year old Black boy, was brutally murdered for allegedly flirting with a white woman. Two white men nearly beat Emmett to death. They gouged out his eyes and shot the boy in the head. Then, they tied Emmett to a cotton-gin fan with barbed wire and threw his lifeless body into the Tallahatchie River. Years later, we witness additional waves of Blacks being murdered because of the color of their skin like, Rayshard Brooks, George Floyd, Breonna Taylor, Atatiana Jeffers, Stephon Clark, Bothham Jean and many other victims of racism and hate. Currently, the time is now 1:05 pm on Wednesday, November 4, 2020. The presidential race to 270 electoral votes is Biden 238 to Trump 213. The suspense of this political race is worrisome because there is so much at stake including race relations in America and the survival of the Black race in general.

In the American political system, race division is evident when you look at and listen to the people who occupy seats in the House of Representatives and the Senate. There really is no concrete distinction between these two political entities. Regardless of your socioeconomic status, if you are Black, step back and if you are white, you are always right. This is evident because the decisions politicians make for the American people are not motivated based on the needs of the American people, but they are inspired by self-greed and self-promotion. You would assume that these government officials would be more focused on correcting a wrong. Yet, how can we as citizens expect for the government to "Do the right thing." That would be too much like right. For Black America, this is a wrong against a race of people who are the foundation of what America has become in the global economy and on the world stage minus its racist history. If the corrupt politicians in America would put aside their selfishness, the world would be a better place for all Americans, especially for Black Americans who have yet to benefit from any policies and political agendas set forth by any political administration. This is the year for democrats and republicans alike to put aside their petty differences and put the people first and at the forefront of their political agenda.

In reality, together we can do virtually anything as a race if we work together for the purpose to ensure that our people are afforded equal opportunity to obtain and live the American Dream. However, so many of us are living an individualized existence because some of us believe in the "All about me mentality." It was never about the individual Black man or woman, but about our entire race as we have been repeatedly shown time after time when we witness police brutality, inequity in education and in the workforce, in housing, and in the financial market. When does it change? When will we change? How can we change? However, nothing will change if we do not take action now. So many Black people don't vote in federal elections, state elections, or municipal elections. They often think that their vote doesn't count, but every vote counts regardless of popular belief of the average non-voter skeptic. In this world, one has to take a chance on faith, and believe that anything is possible if we work hard towards a common goal. The decisions we make in this world are not isolated choices. Unfair as it may sound, we,

Black Americans, are generally stigmatized by our actions and behaviors which impact and affect every man, woman, and child in our race because we will always be judged by our tenets and ideologies.

In truth, regardless of what has been our past, we deserve a better future. As a Black American, I refuse to give up the chance to make an impactful and substantial difference for my race. I know that black is beautiful, black don't crack under pressure, and I truly believe that Black lives can improve through real change in this country, and I also know that Black Lives Do Matter! Those are the truths which I have always and continue to live by as a Black woman living in America. That is why I vote year after year in the general, federal, state and municipal elections. I see myself as a change agent, not a complaint-mongler. If we want change, we have to vote for change until evolution comes into existence. After all, our goal is to establish a new beginning for the Black people living in this country by evoking a future of plentitude and prosperity. When I was a child, I remember seeing so many young Black kids hanging out in the street instead of hitting the books. I would go home after school to see *The*

Brady Bunch and wonder, why aren't the kids in the neighborhood more focused on their future? Looking at life through young eyes, life appears more carefree and innocent, but viewing life through adult eyes one can see the hardships and dangers which emerge in the urban community. With that being said, there is an urgency to renew urban America and revitalize the lives of its citizens.

The decisions we make can be challenging, but not making a decision can prove to be tragic. When Biden received 306 votes compared to Trump's 232, America made her decision to change the economic and social dynamics of this country for the better. When Americans showed up to vote, each individual understood that the casting vote was definitely a decision worth fighting for regardless of the mundane rhetoric Trump was spinning on the eleven o'clock news and on twitter during the late night hours. Even after the election was over, Trump continued with his verbal tirades. With the departure of Trump, it is now out with the old and in with the new presidential administration. We say goodbye to Trump's 99% white cabinet members and in with a diverse presidential cabinet that resembles a multicultural

America. This country was built on the backs of slaves and immigrants. Therefore, those are the people who should be visible in a presidential cabinet if we want to truly be recognized as the United States of America. This country should be based on the ideals of "For the People and By the People" which is the premise of the old adage, "liberty and Justice for All." Those words will only hold true meaning and value when Americans come to realize as stated by former President Barack Obama that, "There is not a Black America, a White America, a Latino America, or an Asian America. There is the United States of America" (Ratcliffe, 2017). Until all Americans come to this realization, there will continue to be chaotic episodes of hate and violence plaguing this country, thus suppressing the Black American.

A New Beginning for Us All

The dreamers and doers of the Black race have paved the way for our future in this country. Their genius, influence, and ingenuity has carved a place for us all in society as a community of competent, creative, and intelligent men and women of color. Mandela, Gundai, King, and Malcolm X were revolutionaries in their own right who contributed to the evolution of change for a race of people. Decades later, we see that their fortitude to bring about equitable change continues to echo in the cities and towns in this country and around the globe. The sheer gravity of their defying actions has catapulted significant advancement opportunities for people of color even in current day America. It was their fierce individual views and beliefs which helped mold the United States of America into a better place to live, but there remains more to be done. Nelson Mandela said it best in a speech that he made after the African National Congress (ANC) election victory, 2 May 1994, which reads, "For we must, together and without delay, begin to build a better life for all South Africans; this means creating jobs, building houses, providing education, and bringing peace and security for all" (p. 149). Those words echoed across the ocean to the United States through the voices of all who believe in equality for all men and women regardless of race or creed.

Comprehensively, it is understandable to conclude how true evolution is based on a nation's willingness to create systemic change that will benefit all of its citizens by forging formidable community relationships among the people. Black Americans in particular need reassurance that their lives matter, and that their children are safe growing up in the country they were born in. Moreover, Black families need to know they can go about their daily lives without having to worry about being murdered for being a person of color. These old ways of thinking and being projected to the world must be revamped. Little Black boys and girls should not have to say, "I want to live." Life is a God giving right bestowed upon all living things, especially human beings. The 2020 presidential election represents a new beginning for all of us. Each year our lives should represent another success, a new accomplishment, new life, or a new perspective on life.

There should never be a stand-still in reference to our productivity level. With each day brings another chance for hope and an inkling of change. Life and opportunity is something every person living on this planet is entitled to as a human being. Keep in mind that the only limitations are the ones we place on ourselves, or those limitations we allow others to place on us.

In order to establish a new beginning in the United States of America for all Black Americans, there must be diversity at all levels of government, in the private sector, and in the business sector as well before any shifts in economics can truly be obtained or established for the Black American citizen. From our professional, business, social, and political platforms, we must give voice to those who cannot speak for themselves. Defend those who cannot fight for themselves, and help those who cannot think for themselves. There are so many people crying for help in this country who are not being heard. It astounds me how the United States government gets richer while its people get poorer. This is a country with enormous wealth. There should not be excessive unemployment and extensive homeless rates in this nation. It is time for

America to spread the wealth among its people. Hopefully, this new presidential administration will break the "glass ceiling" by making global and national history by creating financial equity for the people by the people. We all know about those redundant political promises made during the election campaign, but the people need words of truth, and words of integrity from the incoming administration. Enough is enough! The American people need to see real change in 2021 within the first 100 days of public office.

Unfortunately, for the Black race, change is a word that we have heard repeatedly drift from the mouths of many republican and democratic leaders of government. This current state of the country is reflective of the words of James Baldwin who in his own right was a master of word play. Baldwin once stated in an essay called *Notes of A Native Son* that, "... it is galling now to be pitied as a victim, to accept this ready sympathy which is limited only by its failure to accept him as an American" (p. 88). James Baldwin's words epitomize the unfortunate reality that although born and raised in America, the Black American continues to be degraded and viewed as a second class citizen in his native land. It does not matter how many deaths we hear about on the nightly news or how many spouts of racial injustice we experience in this world, in the words of Langston Hughes, Black America will always have to fight for a seat at the table. Our current fight for a new exordium is just beginning because systemic racism is deeply rooted in the American soil. The politician can preach, give a perfect speech, and continue to make promises, but nothing will change if the negative and biased political stance in this country is not modified or altered. Words are just words until the meaning of those words have been expressed thoroughly through action.

Our New Beginning

The responsibility and expectations fall within our own hands. We need not continue to place our confidence and beliefs in the palms of the politician regardless of the political party. Some people place their faith in republicans while others believe in the democratic leaders. As a Black American female, I only see the politician; the false prophet, or the unruly one. Until these leaders prove worthy, I will remain neutral. Just this past year, I have observed the deep division of this country to a level of absurdity. How can people be so hateful? Why did Trump have to encourage and promote hate in this country when so many civil rights leaders, politicians, and American citizens worked so diligently to calm the waters of hatred? These are a few questions which have emerged in my mind from the Trump presidency which have caused a serious issue in America. This current administration has managed to destroy a century of progress and annihilate our collective efforts for equality. This may technically be the year 2020, but it seems like the 1950s and 1960s in reference to the level of racial incidents I have been reading about in the news, or had the unfortunate opportunity to view on social media. When will this madness end I wonder?

Truth be told, it may never truly end. There are various beliefs in this world regarding human nature. The following statements represent those beliefs. One belief is, "You cannot move forward with your life unless you know where you came from." Another rudimentary belief is, "You must know who you are before you can find your right path in life." Each of these statements encompasses the theme regarding identity. If identity is based on the environment in which we live, and the people we encounter in life, what is to be said about a group of people being stripped of their true purpose in life through the process of oppressive tactics such as systemic racism and social injustice. Do those practices sound equitable? Do those practices seem productive for the oppressed? As I witness repeated news segments of Trump questioning the voting process in this country by undermining the American people and the political system in general, it makes me nauseous to think that this man was ever the leader of this country. How naive so many people were to trust this political impostor. Knowing that a significant number of people who voted for Trump in the 2020 election were Black Americans is another bafflement I am not attempting to contemplate at this juncture in time regardless of how disturbing that reality may be.

However, if our new beginning stems from our past, what have we as Americans truly learned from our past indiscretions in this country? Do we really want our history to repeat itself, or are we ready and willing to write a new, progressive, fair, and equitable chapter for all

Americans, especially for the Black American. Personally, I have always believed in the possibility of seeing equitable forms of educational, professional, and financial equity during my lifetime as a Black person born and raised in America. Being a Black female with a Philosophical Doctrine (PhD) would be viewed as an example of progressive change since I grew up in urban America. But, that can be viewed as an isolated event. In order for significant change to be established in America for Blacks, each Black child must be afforded a fair, appropriate, and public education that stems from equitable opportunities that are not limited to just a few. There has to exist a real representation of value in the education system. The philosophical door of academic excellence must be open to all races of people, specifically Black America. Within this ideal learning paradigm there would be no exclusions, and technological and STEM assets would be provided to each child who aspires to obtain a quality rich and productive education regardless of race or creed.

Equitable advancement in education has to become our new normal if we expect to see any fruits from our labor. Be mindful that no one can stop us now because we had enough of nothing. Now we want to see and experience a lot of everything this country has to offer that will benefit us as American citizens reaching towards the true ideals of the American Dream.

CHAPTER 10:
Creating a New Vision

Black America, do we dare acknowledge that the spoils of injustice, anarchy, discontent, and hatred are all around us and embedded within our wound as a race of people? Or, is this just a metaphorical allusion? Whatever the case may be, we as a group must understand that it is our responsibility and charge to create a new vision for the Black race because what we have been doing over the past few decades has not brought about equitable change outcomes for our race. Maintaining our heritage, and manufacturing a new vision for our race has to begin somewhere, so why not start here. First let's start by acknowledging that we must have ownership in our own communities. There is no way the rest of the world will start to respect what we have to say if we don't start taking care of ourselves. Second let's revisit how we are being educated and let's take control of properly educating ourselves and especially our youth, in order to do that we have to really take a look at the definition of education. Third, our economy, we have to start focusing on our cash flow, we can not continue to spend billions and trillions of dollars with people who frankly totally disregard our needs. Tell me, have you seen the corner store owner in a Black neighborhood with a Black Lives Matter sign up as they march with the protesters, and the sad part is after we (Black people) finish demanding our civil rights, it is people like the corner store owner who benefits the most from our plight. He benefits the most because we won't take advantage of the opportunities that are brought about because of our plight.

In order to consummate our vision for the future, we must have goals and purpose. Each goal requires having a strategic plan. Therefore, we have to first recognize and accept the fact that obtaining financial ownership of our own Black communities will increase our financial wealth and the livelihood of our families. The antiquated phrase "It takes money to make money" holds true even today. Money flowing in our communities will increase property values and create better work opportunities for our community members. Acknowledgement is the initial step involved in progression. This makes me think of the actions of the fictional movie character George Bailey in the film *"It's A Wonderful Life"* portrayed by legendary Hollywood actor James Stewart. The main character George Bailey sacrifices his future plans, dreams, and aspirations for the betterment of the community. This fictional character was willing to put his blood, sweat, and tears into building up the lives of every citizen within his neighborhood. If not for the generosity of this character, so many people would have been homeless and unemployed. The actions of that character demonstrated great sacrifice and commitment to excellence.

Even though George Bailey is a fictitious character in a movie, the behaviors of that particular character resonate within the hearts of each man and woman who believes in human survival, goodwill towards all men, and charity. In this world, we must determine what our actual purpose in life is as it applies to contributing to the world in which we live. Are we to just eat and sleep? Or, should we create change to benefit the greater good of people within our communities? There is no place for selfishness in this world. For the life we truly want to experience, we must be clear in our intent and purposeful in our collective actions. Knowing that it takes a working class man years to save $5,000, working as a community, it would only take us a matter of weeks to produce $500, 000 to purchase two blocks of houses. This is based on the vision of changing Black renters into Black homeowners. Everyone deserves to live comfortably regardless of their socioeconomic status. In *It's A Wonderful Life,* the premise of the main character's life was to serve his community by increasing environmental wealth for all of the community members while going up against the elite. If not for the persistence and assertiveness of George Bailey, the citizens of Bedford Falls would have become poverty-stricken and homeless.

This is confirmation that just like in the movies, in the real-world, the decisions we make can either negatively or positively impact the community in which we live. Neighborhoods flourish when the people living within them contribute to the community. Without equity in a neighborhood, it cannot thrive and its community members cannot excel. Cities such as Baltimore and Detroit are viewed as two of the most dangerous cities in the world, but this is mainly due to the lack of economic prosperity and career opportunity. Working in Baltimore City, I often witness the carnage taking place within this urban area. Moreover, I see how so many citizens of Baltimore have been stripped of basic privileges such as completing high school, venturing into college, obtaining a career paying job, and being afforded decent housing. As it relates to unfortunate circumstances, we know that the rich get richer and the poor become poorer. However, on the other side of that spectrum, when people begin to see beyond themselves and direct their efforts to improving the lives of others including their neighbors their own lives become richer and more meaningful.

Ice Cube said it best when he mentioned his personal and political views regarding how there should be a contract for Black America. His ideals are not politically based or motivated as most may believe, but rather grounded on historical fact. In this country, "The American Dream" is just that for many Black people. It has been nothing but a dream, or a baseless foundation in which nothing has developed or come to fruition, especially when there continues to be a massive wealth gap in Black America compared to White America. It is the actions of those in power such as the republicans and democrats in addition to the President of the United States who have ignored the economic plight of Black Americans for decades in this country. Black suffrage in America can be traced back to the tragic and devastating days of slavery, or witnessed today by repeated acts of police brutality and social injustice across this divided country. For the average Black family, expecting them to have the monetary means to save for a home may prove unreachable in a country where financial and economic opportunity is unequally distributed among the people. However, for Black America, the goal is to ensure that our people have someplace to grow, work, and advance academically, professionally, and financially opposed to crawling to the "white man" for public assistance.

Our Intrinsic and Extrinsic Motivation

When is the right time to improve the depleting socioeconomic status of the Black race? Slavery in America began in 1619 and ended in 1865, yet in the current year of 2020 there has been an overwhelming emergence of Jim

Crow behavior within the American culture, justice, and the political systems. This is a precedent that we as Black Americans denounce. These actions we have been observing and experiencing in current day America are a betrayal of the American social and justice system, and a reflection of the decapitating reality of the human rights system in which men and women in this country have fought for over a course of many decades. Now we are witnessing a major disruption in this nation that is being observed by American allies and enemies alike. When our enemies see a country divided, they also observe a country revealing its vulnerabilities, insecurities, and it's inconsistencies. With that being said, that which motivates us to turn on each other and divide us based on red or blue or black or white is a form of insanity. It would be imprudent, reckless, and absurd to accept this current reality in our society. As Black Americans, we as a race, refuse to be dismissed as human beings and denied the opportunities we deserve as a people.

Reflecting on chapters 1 through 8, it is imperative that we reflect on both our intrinsic and extrinsic motivation to encourage us all in changing the educational, professional, and economic dynamics of the Black race within this country. We must be the encouragers for our own race, the supporters of our own blood, and the protectors of our own minds. Year after year in America, we witness the same social, political, financial, and economic injustice that continues to destroy and oppress us as a race. Fair and even levels of equity are currently non-existent in this country between the Black and White race. As an American, I always hoped that this would be the very factor that would motivate us collectively to develop a plan to even the professional and financial playing field in this country. Knowing that "race" is a profound word within itself, the question remains, what do we think of when we use the word? I think of someone competing for a position and usually that position is first place. Well, it's no different when you talk about race in America. Everyone is competing for a position, Black people (in America) seem to be the only people that do not recognize it. If this is not true, then tell me why Asians do business with Asians? Do you believe one of those Chinese stores would buy food from a Black food distributor with very low prices? No! Of course not, because they understand that it is a race, a group race, not an individual race. Money is nothing if it doesn't produce power, influence, opportunity, and self-respect. At least it is not much when speaking about long term effects.

Basically, the opportunity to change the educational, financial, and economic course of our people is now. We must be tactical and mindful of our needs. First let's deal with why, Black people, at least some of us who are descendants of slaves, are here in the first place. That reason can be summed up in one word, Capitalism, which I have developed a very strange love-hate relationship for, the word and the ideology itself. So, if capitalism is the reason we are here, then we should use capitalism to empower our Black nation. Second, what does an empowered Black nation in America look like? In short, what is it? How do we live? What are our standards? How do we make and distribute our funds? What do we contribute to the system that sets us apart? These questions and many more have to be analyzed and answered with confidence and conviction that this is our path to regain our position in this world as African Kings and Queens and not allow ourselves to continue to be underrepresented and marginalized in a capitalistic society.

Capitalism

Since the days of slavery, the rights, freedoms and liberties of Black people have been capsized. Every time Blacks make progress that progress gets overturned. This is due to the capitalistic society we have been thrusted into since birth. The principles of White America are not based on the needs of Black America. Those philosophies are solely based on the succession of the "white race." When certain ideologies focus mainly on supporting a singular race of people, the rest of the population becomes marginalized. In truth, the principles of capitalistic attitudes regarding equality in the United States of America have always been geared towards the extinction of the Black race and the progressiveness of White America. Even in current day society, wealth opportunities for large portions of the Black race are scarce or non-existent. It is difficult to admit that most Black citizens are living a mediocre life which has become commonplace in

American society due to the lack of educational and financial opportunities afforded to our specific group. For the Black race, the concept of inequality is a very real phenomenon which exists within our Black communities. Although we are the occupants, we are not the ones capitalizing from the fruits of our own labor. It is the housing capital which brings about the financial capital that "slum-lords" gross from the assets they have within these Black communities. After all, the real-estate monopoly is a "white-man's" playground. This is simply a way for them to liquidate-wealth which they use to capitalize on the Black population by taking advantage of the entire financial market and restricting Blacks from gaining momentum in these conventional "Wall Street" resource avenues.

Depleting resources for the Black family has been taking a serious and devastating nose-dive, especially between the years of 2017 and 2020. Donald Trump's presidency has been nothing but a catastrophe for the American people, but more so for Black Americans in general. The past four years with Trump has been a total collision. We have been bombarded with a series of repeated social unrest due to massive hate crimes against our race, being denied social justice from politicians on both sides of the aisle in addition to a slew of police involved shootings which have been excused by a corrupt judicial system. Not only have we been protesting and fighting for equality during these past four years, we have been fighting for equality throughout the course of our entire lives. Is it unreasonable to expect a president or commander in chief of the country in which we live to represent all Americans, or are we expected to not see ourselves as American born citizens? These questions anger me because we are Americans, and we deserve and are entitled to fair treatment and respect like our white counterparts. Yet, we continue to reside in a country that does not acknowledge, appreciate, or value us as natural-born-citizens. As mentioned earlier in chapter one, family is our "Bedrock." Therefore, it is our charge and obligation to our families and communities to persevere in the face of adversity as we attempt to change the current course of Black life in an America fueled with such hatred and political discourse.

Considering how precious family and resources are we must take a stance and hold ourselves and the people who govern our society to a higher standard. Let's do away with the traditional and past verbal discourse which was always filled with empty promises to the American people, especially towards the Black American population. This is basically the middle-of-the-road for all of America. There is no going backwards on this journey. We have to pursue the dreams of our fathers and mothers, and their descendants before them had for their children and their children's children. Personally, I have heard enough complaints, excuses, and promises to last me a lifetime. When I see my reflection in the mirror of life, I see a strong, competent, creative, capable and assertive Black woman. Therefore, I stand for bringing about tangible, concrete, visible and actual change to urban communities and the Black race in particular. As an American citizen, I refuse to listen to anymore rhetoric from republicans and democrats who are famous for playing the blame-game. I want action for the Black race, and I want it now. Enough with the political discourse and obscenities this is the time to promote systemic change for Black Americans by creating systemic financial opportunities for the Black minority.

An Empowered Black Nation

In reality, Black brotherhood is not an illusion, especially not in the United States of America in the year 2020. For the Black American, too much has happened and too little has been done to rectify and resolve the social unjust and unrest we have experienced throughout the course of our lives in this country. There have been too many incidents and events which have stripped "The Black Man" of his dignity, pride, respect, livelihood, and in many cases robbed him of his life. On that disturbing note, we must consider the concept of empowering ourselves as citizens of this nation, a nation in which infringement continues to be the norm when considering the needs of the Black American. The action of limiting and undermining the progression of the Black race continues to be the goal of the republic. Instead of existing within a true democracy, we, the Black American, find ourselves drawing breath within a nation where there is no room to breathe. Therefore, today and in the years to come, Black Americans must become an empowered group as we once were during the time of the Slavery Revolts of the 1800s and the Civil Rights Movement of the 1950s and 1960s. Like our forefathers and foremothers, we have the ability to free ourselves from societal restraints and economic bondage and overcome any obstacles which restrict us from excelling educationally and financially in this world.

The goal is to become nationally empowered by educating ourselves, our children, and the people living within our Black communities, so that they can successfully compete for jobs in science, technology, engineering and mathematics. Gone are the days of the Black laymen. This is the preamble for "Black Men Rising." As a race, we must confirm that we have the right to start a free republic which enables us to truly obtain educational and financial equity within the American system. These are rights and privileges which we must demand and aspire to achieve as a community because those ideals have never been given to us willingly. Moreover, these are societal shifts we must institute as a race if we expect for compensatory change to actually occur within our lifetime while living in this current state of corruption. From a socioeconomic perspective, we cannot afford to wait any longer. As I reflect on the senseless deaths of George Floyd, Breonna Taylor, and other Black citizens who have lost their lives to some tragic, unlawful, and criminal manmade assault on Black citizens, I am greatly disturbed by the fact that the taking of Black life continues to be such a casual occurrence. The American flag is supposed to symbolize humanity and brotherhood as it waves in the day's breeze, but within this Black soul, I feel no relief. I continue to be displeased by the rhetoric of those who continue to lead this nation down the road of uncertainty and across the bridge of death.

Becoming an empowered nation within a nation may be our only recourse as Black Americans, especially when our voices continue to be ignored and our lives continue to be taken on a whim. To dismiss the fact that Black lives are being eradicated would be rash to say the least. As we head towards 2021 and beyond, we must turn our sights on a new evolution. Therefore, Black America must embrace this coming year as "The Year of Change."

Keep in mind that brotherhood is not something to take likely because it involves forging strength in numbers as well as creating strength in finances. From the dawn of time, nations have been built on lifelong relationships with allies who have common interests with those seeking refuge and progression in the new world. Those same ideologies have merit even today. Black historians like Deborah C. Wright, Edward Wyckoff Willkiams, Maggie Lena Walker, Dwight Lamar Bush Sr., Emma C.Chappell, P.W. Chavers, Robert Reed Church Sr., and Dana A. Dorsey are well-known entrepreneurs, bankers, businessmen and women who rose to the hierarchical peak of the financial market in America. Regardless of how many obstacles they may have faced, these Black men and women focused their sites on progressive change in the financial industry for Black Americans and managed to succeed.

Reflecting on their efforts and accomplishments, we realize that, as Black Americans, we will always find ourselves being pushed-back by the opposition, but it is our responsibility to push back and keep it moving. Dreams remain dreams when there is no purpose and action. However, on the other side of that spectrum, dreams become reality when we take a stand and remain steadfast in our pursuit for "liberty and justice for all." As we seek to create an upward paradigm shift in this current financial market for Black America, we must think bigger by building a wealth- legacy and not just settle for a temporary fix because for too long Black Americans have missed out on educational and financial opportunities that their white counterparts have been relishing for centuries. In order to build generational wealth, we must include this concept into our long-term financial goals. Getting out of debt and saving money are just the bare essentials to financial freedom. The meat of financial wealth is contingent upon our ability to ensure that we have the educational and financial resources and the business savvy to past down a significant amount of wealth from one generation to the next. This is how we become financially empowered as a race.

Let's face it, the color of money is green, not black or white. Green represents growth and prosperity. It symbolizes strength in one's lineage. Furthermore, the color green encompasses the background in which we build our lives upon, the African heritage which we represent as a race, and the roots in which the blood from our ancestors flow throughout our veins. Moving forward in our pursuit, when we think about our family, we must also think about the dynasty which we want to leave behind to prevent our children's children from living in poverty. That is why building generational wealth is such a long term goal. It references succession regarding monetary wealth, stocks, real estate property, and monumental riches which emerge from obtaining a high quality education, social networking and long term investments. This is about capitalizing off of reusable sustainability. In layman's terms, it is a scaffolding process in which you are able to leave behind financial resources which come in the form of real estate assets, use the genetic skills, traits, and talents inherited from your parents, provide the educational knowledge your children can carry on into the future and teach their children, and/or pass on a series of profitable stock market strategies your children can use to obtain future wealth. Regardless of your temperament for business and education, know that your legacy should bring great reward to your family and their families after them.

In light of everything that has been happening in the United States of America, Black unity is a major topic we need to consider as we reframe the financial situation that plagues our communities. This is not an "I Thing," this is an "Us Thing." The proverbial "survival of the fittest" as we begin our reign of change by ensuring that our children pursue and receive an elite college education as mentioned in chapter 4 of this book. From both a philosophical and a biological perspective I profited from my parentage. I was able to extract creativity, money sense, style, world insight, and fortitude from both of my parents. There is something to be said about extraction of parental genes. I guess you can say, "I lucked out!" In the same way we get our physical characteristics from our parents, we inherit their cognitive functions as well. Looking back on my path in life, I see that the genealogy I derived from my mother and father got me to this educational and financial juncture in my life. The wealth of knowledge and skill sets I have inherited from my parents will be passed down to my children and their children's children. I have created a proud heritage for my family, and I take stock in all of my achievements which were bestowed upon me through my bloodline. It is that same sense of family and community which we as Black Americans must cling to while becoming an empowered nation within a wider nation.

Living a Meaningful and Purposeful Life

The overall goal for the Black American is to live a meaningful life with purpose because a life without purpose is an empty void which represents a vacuum of nothingness. As a race, we have worked too hard and too long to accept anything less than prosperity. This entails creating better schools in underserved communities, affording those living in urban areas jobs paying a living wage, and expanding career and financial opportunities for minorities in general. Knowing that each year brings forth new opportunities for individual progression, Black Americans have to embrace the concept that anything is possible in regards to establishing educational and economic equity in America. Moreover, as Black

Americans, we have to ensure "fairness and inclusion" are the principles and priorities being established in our public school institutions. Ensuring that Black boys and girls are able to achieve the highest level of academic excellence must be at the forefront of our educational and political agenda. It takes a village to raise a child, and we are the villagers within our communities who are positioned to improve the academic circumstance of the Black student.

In reference to obtainment of economic equity, the current state of financial wealth for many Black Americans is basically nonexistent. After the Great Recession which began in 2007 and ended in 2009, systemic financial inequality between Black and White Americans widened significantly. In that, the measure of an individual and his or her family net worth is based on the financial opportunities afforded to them in an already rigged financial system, especially regarding people of color. When Black Americans are provided substantial financial opportunities, they are afforded the means to live a purposeful and meaningful life. On the other hand, when these opportunities are limited or absent from the equation, there is no equity or financial gain.

Distribution of Funds

In a corrupt financial system, fairness in funding distribution is often a non-factor especially in Black, urban communities. From a monetary perspective, in the real-world money matters because it is one of the most important resources in this country. If financial systems within the United States of America are not placing urban education and community based homeownership at the center of their agenda regarding community involvement, members of the community cannot progress exponentially. It is a given that increased funding in underserved communities leads to greater and improved educational resources which are beneficial to students attending urban schools specifically. As community members, we must effectively analyze how state funding is being allocated to public schools, and we should communicate with state officials to ensure that urban students are benefiting academically from use of those funds.

Even though the cost of education may vary based on the geographic location of schools, providing equal opportunity education for all students regardless of race or creed should be the same. Sure enough, "The effective use of education funding can lead to adequate staffing of schools; a full, rich curriculum; and effective class sizes, all of which can improve student outcomes" (Baker, Farrie & Sciarra, p. 7). Considering how so many urban schools are failing at massive rates, it is imperative to change the proverbial narrative by making a public commitment to these institutions of learning. Creating a new vision starts with the children. We have to make life-long learning accessible to students attending these urban schools, so they are able to matriculate successfully into higher education and the workforce.

The New Black Vision

The vicious cycle regarding racism and wealth inequality in America continues to rear its ugly head. At times, it seems as if there is no recourse for the Black American. However, as a unified group with a common purpose we can change the education, career and wealth dynamics of this current and unjust society we find ourselves enthralled in today. The anarchy which has emerged throughout the year 2020 due to the rhetoric of an unstable and unethical president has shifted not only American politics, but dimmed American trust. We are a country divided now more than ever. Therefore, the only way to ensure that the Black population obtains a piece of the philosophical "American Dream" is to generate "A New Black Vision." It is either now or never if we expect to provide economic wealth and security for our children and our children's children.

Like a mighty closed-fist, the power, strength, and the very foundation of Black life was built on sisterhood and brotherhood. Historically, Black organizations like *The Black Panthers, the Black Male Voter Project, Black Women's Blueprint,* and *The National Association for the*

Advancement of Colored People (NAACP) have instituted social practices and programs to support and protect the welfare of the Black American. Even today the *Black Lives Matter Movement* and *Black PAC* organizations are continuing with the traditions for addressing social and economic injustice against Blacks in America. These organizations are the very fiber and backbone we depend upon when considering which direction we need to follow in our pursuit of educational and economic equity.

In our collective pursuit as a race, we understand that for every action, there will always be a reaction from the Black community regarding our rights as American citizens, especially when those rights are being violated and stripped away by racist radicals. It is at this point that we become true visionaries for our own people. Knowing how we, Black Americans, are viewed as a race underestimated by most, and disregarded and ignored by others is appalling and un-American. Once the Trump presidency ended, that was our cue to reestablish ourselves as citizens entitled to *"Life, Liberty, and the Pursuit of Happiness"* as indicated in the United States Declaration of Independence. These are words we hold true as protections regarding our God given and legal rights as naturally born citizens of the United States of America.

Race Recourse

When it comes to defining race and racism in this country, we can reflect on American history both past and recent. It is a known fact that race and racism have always divided social and political outcomes in this country. Jefferson once said, "The first difference that strikes us is that of colour." Unfortunately, those words hold true even today. As we, Black Americans proceed with changing the educational and financial dynamics of our people, keep in mind that the hallmark of the history of race in our country has always been against us instead of in support of us. Skepticism can never be a variable in our plans moving forward in this divided democracy. It is only through sheer optimism and fortitude that Black America will be able to obtain true equity in all aspects of life. Malcolm X said it best when he stated that, "Nobody can give you freedom. Nobody can give you equality or justice or anything. If you're a man, you take it." Through his words, I am inspired to take action by using my voice and my professional platform to educate Black Americans on what needs to be done to ensure that we are able to create and leave a source of generational wealth behind for our Black families and communities.

By Reflecting on our past history in the United States of America as a race, we can ascertain what we need to change to forge a better and quality future for ourselves and our families. This requires us to supersede pessimism in order for our communities to thrive and function as a united and unwavering vessel of hope. Within each pocket of our urban communities men, women, and children aspire to excel in life by acquiring some aspect of the American Dream. We have the charge as community members to support and help maintain the aspirations of our community members by being a strong voice and a political advocate that echoes across America. It will be our collective actions as a group which will establish the comprehensive agenda we must initiate to fulfill our goal to reach the levels of wealth and financial security as our white counterparts have taken pleasure in for centuries in America.

Being apprehensive about life and the lives of our people is something that has been a constant in the life of the Black American. These are not baseless comments, but concerning statements that emerge from real-world events in our history. Within the United States, Black lives are under siege in the sense that in the year 2020 racism incited by racist politicians and those in power surrounding our communities place restrictive barriers which cut off the essential supplies and monetary aid urban America needs to flourish and survive. Without oxygen we cannot live or breathe, and without equal opportunity we cannot advance as a people. As a true visionary, a woman, a mother, a daughter, a sister, an aunt, and especially as a Black American, the actions of racist America stripping the rights and dignity of the Black race is an unconscionable action that is depraved and unethical. Therefore, educating Black communities and Black Americans in general on the urgency in changing the social, economic, and financial dynamics of their lives is a crucial and necessary call for action.

Community Involvement

Ensuring that the people within our communities have peace of mind, obtain homeownership, and can reach a comfortable level of financial security is an important aspect of the American Dream. This initiative requires us to become more involved in community affairs. Not as a mouthpiece, but as a real change agent because the future of our race depends on our sincere efforts to educate our people. This means building lifelong relationships with community members, putting in the time and effort in rebuilding our Black communities, and promoting a rich heritage and legacy built on pride and stewardship. These efforts are not about compensation for our actions, but commitment to our communities.

When I speak with citizens within urban communities, I notice how the consensus is that they want more for themselves and their families, but do not fully understand how to go about making those changes in their lives. As I mentioned earlier in this book, my personal experiences regarding community involvement as a child set the stage for my educational and professional journey in life. The men and women working at those recreation centers provided resources for me and other children within our community to excel and strive in school. They provided us with a sense of structure and community which encouraged us to go to college, become homeowners, and give back to our community through good works and deeds. It is apparent to me that the foundation of real change starts in the home and extends into the community. Change is having the ability to alter, vary, or modify someone's life through purpose. However, the process of change requires one to make a real difference in the world which amounts to substantial growth in community. Educators are known for changing and enriching the lives of children because they teach them the skills and strategies they need to sustain themselves in life. Yet, over the past few decades, Black boys and girls in urban American communities have not reached exponential levels of achievement due to the lack or absence of funding required to propel their educational experience to that of students being taught in private and county schools. This is an obvious disadvantage which continues to plague the Black community.

This leads us to question, do we really know how much is at stake when we talk about community involvement, or are we just going with the flow while walking blindly down a dark and dismal tunnel? The truth is that community involvement deals with becoming an active decision maker. In that, we are charged with empowering others to use their voices to bring about meaningful and effectual change while knowing our actions will greatly impact their lives forever. This type of commitment requires accountability beyond measure. As Black Americans, we must realize that the behaviors of a community can either impede or advance our collective goals. Therefore, we all must be willing to become advocates for the Black race in the sense that we are representatives for the change we demand in this country. During the course of the next few years, Black America will have more opportunities than we can imagine. The tides are turning in our favor, and we have the authority to redirect the course of our collective journey in a nation divided, but full and rich with possibilities.

Creating a New Vision

Every vision is based on a set of core values. In colleges those values are contained within the college or university's Mission and Vision statements. Within the societal paradigm, those core values emerge from our sense of community, fellowship, and brotherhood. Listening to the voices of our brothers and sisters echo across America calling for change, those of us with the educational, professional, and celebrity platforms must speak up and let our voices be heard across the sea. We need to take a deliberate course of action to ensure that today ends the suffrage, indignations, and inequities Black America has been subjected to for centuries in this country.

As Black Americans, being disenfranchised deprives us of the very essence and privileges associated with the American Dream. Thus, preventing or taking away educational and career opportunities which would enable Black Americans to obtain generational wealth. We must put a stop to police brutality, cease discrimination practices in education, end inequity in the workforce, and increase financial equity for Black Americans in the banking system. Therefore, to overcome racial injustice in America, Black Americans have to disassemble racism and social injustice in our schools, the political system, and cleanse these elements from our communities. Our agenda for promoting such change must be based on the following core values:

1. Demand for Racial Justice
2. Promote a Call for Action through Community Involvement
3. Institute Collective Bargaining regarding the Financial System in this country
4. Demand Fair and Equal Opportunity in Education
5. End Discrimination in the Workforce
6. Demand for Equal and Fair Housing Opportunities in Affluent Neighborhoods

The bottom line is our actions must be forceful and deliberate if effectual change is to emerge within this country. We must demand and enforce change, and we must start now. Reflecting on the years to come, we have to realize that within this new realm of possibilities comes forth opportunity and change that can redirect the course of the lives of many Black Americans, especially if we are successful in our actions moving forward. As mentioned by James Baldwin (1984), "It seems to be typical of life in America, where opportunities, real and fancied, are thicker than anywhere else on the globe, that the second generation has no time to talk to the first" (p. 63). Therefore, regardless of what roadblocks come our way, we have to institute a new way of living for the Black race by creating a new vision based on educational and economic equity. Keep in mind that today represents tomorrow and tomorrow represents the future. In the words of Dr. Martin Luther King, "We will overcome," especially once we as a race begin to forge new and much more positive experiences for the Black man living in America.

Knowing that this current year brought so many challenges, deaths, and destruction to Black America, we cannot turn back now, nor can we be hesitant in our collective actions as a people. Instead, we must take ownership that we are our own change agents, and start planting seeds of consciousness into the minds of our people, especially the young Black boys and girls growing up in our urban communities. Since the future of the Black race depends on the youth, we have to nurture our young like a gardener tends to a bamboo tree. Let us give them the attention that is needed with discipline and the faith of saints, knowing it is our duty to place them on the right path in life. It is ironic to think about how America is known as "The Promised Land," yet in a corrupt, racist, and capitalistic system of government, America has yet to commit to any promises made to the Black American people.

A Message from the Authors

We sincerely hope that you appreciated the information contained within this text, *Establishing Educational and Economic Equity*. As Black Americans, we should never underestimate our worth in this country. We must always realize that this country was built on the backs of our ancestors, and that like them we too are worthy of greatness. It is through great sacrifice that we, as Black Americans, continue to strive towards obtaining educational and economic equity for our entire race. This is a journey covered in the blood, sweat, and tears of many Black Americans who have died in the year 2020 and many decades before them who have lost their lives to social injustice at the hands of brutal and racist police officers and white supremacist who felt the need to end a Black life.

It is the hope of the authors of this book that you are able to put some of these suggestions for obtaining educational and economic equity into practice. Know that you and your family deserve better, and you have the innate ability to reach excellence on multiple levels. This can either be academic excellence by becoming a college graduate and career professional. It can be your ability to become financially situated through real estate investments, or your ability to become a community leader and positively change the lives of our Black youths and place them on the road to success.

In the end, we all need to have a common vision, as a race of people we need to understand how important it is for each one to teach one. We are in this together. Please, aspire to contribute to helping our Black communities prosper and become exceedingly productive because Black Lives Do Matter! Let us keep in mind that there is a need for great change in the Black community. We hope you all will become advocates in your community. That is how we will bring about an evolution. We hope the chapters in this book were inspiring in one way or another. Furthermore, we hope that the words in this book were beneficial to you in some special way.

Acknowledgments

Mr. Harris and I are extremely grateful for this opportunity to share and reflect on various societal topics which motivated us to write and publish this book. Establishing Educational and Economic Equity is a major topic which has been evident in the American public sector as well as in its political system for centuries. At various points while composing this text, so many people have expressed to us that we should work together on a book project to voice our ideas and opinions about the current state of our country and how those events are negatively impacting Black Americans. Those suggestions catapulted our decision to write about the ideals for changing the educational and financial dynamic of the Black male and female living in this nation.

Our deepest gratitude is extended to all of those who believe in the Black Lives Matter Movement and understand how in order for the American economy to truly be a representation of all Americans, fairness, opportunity, and equity at each level of the academic, professional, and financial hierarchy must be a reality and not a farce. This is a universal concept because Black Lives extend across the world. It does not matter if you are born in America or elsewhere, know that if you are a person of African descent your life does and will always matter!

As always, a writer is aware of the time it takes composing a written work and how that time can be a strain on the family. With that being said, we both want to give thanks to God for getting us through this tireless process, and thank our families for supporting our time away from them on this philosophical and spiritual journey called writing. Despite how much time we had to dedicate to this project, we truly believe that the time and effort we put into this project was worth the end result.

About the Authors

Dr. Lisa R. Washington has been an educator for Baltimore City Public Schools since 1995. She has taught elementary, middle school, and high school students during her instructional career. Dr. Washington has worn many different hats in her profession. She has been a classroom teacher, a Reading Specialist, a Special Educator, a Mentor Teacher, an Intervention Teacher, a Middle School Mathematics Teacher, a Lead Teacher for Summer Learning Programs, an English Instructor, an Instructional Support Teacher (IST), and an Instructional Coach. Dr. Washington worked as an Adjunct Professor in the English and Humanities Department at Baltimore City Community College from 2005-2011. In addition to her teaching career, Dr. Washington is the author of *A Quantitative Study on Student Engagement at Achieving the Dream and Non-Achieving the Dream Community Colleges Evaluated with CCSSE Data, The Dawn of Time, However You May Wish To Interpret Me, The Seasons of Change,* and *A Matter of Perspective: A Philosophical and Poetic View of Life Death and Relationships.* Dr. Washington is still committed to educating the boys and girls of Baltimore City Schools. Her books can be found online at Barnes and Noble at https://www.barnesandnoble.com/ and Amazon at https://www.amazon.com, or you can follow her on Instagram @drlisarwashington.

Mr. Jeremiah N. Harris is the co-founder of *Run My City*. He has been advocating for Black youth for over ten years. Mr. Harris was born in Baltimore, Maryland. He continues to actively support urban youths through actions and deeds. Mr. Harris has been a valued member of *Run My City*. For the past several years, Mr. Harris and the Run My City Program have made a major impact on the lives of young Black boys and girls living in Baltimore City. Run My City is a community based organization which focuses on using sports, education, and leadership initiatives to advocate for Black youths in urban America. Mr. Harris can be contacted at https://www.instagram.com/run_my_city/.

Glossary

Accumulate
To gather or acquire an increasing number or quality of something.

Adage
A proverb or short statement expressing a general truth.

American Dream
The ideal by which equality of opportunity is available to any American, allowing the highest aspirations and goals to be achieved.

Analogous
Comparable in certain respects, typically in a way which makes clearer the nature of the things compared.

Assertive
Having or showing a confident and forceful personality.

Authentic
Meaning of an undisputed origin; genuine.

Bedrock
Meaning to be presented as a solid rock.
Bylaws

A rule made by a company or society to control the actions of its members.

Capital
Meaning wealth in the form of money or other assets owned by a person or organization or available or contributed for a particular purpose such as starting a company or investing in real estate.

Capitalize
To take the chance to gain advantage from something or an opportunity.

Capitalistic
Supporting or based on the principles of capitalism.

Capsize
Meaning to overturn.

Community
A group of people living in the same place or having a particular characteristic in common.

Competency
The ability to do something successfully or efficiently.

Conceptualize
To form a concept or ideas of something.

Creed

A system of Christian or other religious belief; a faith.

Curriculum

The subjects comprising a course of study in a school or college.

Cynicism

An inclination to believe that people are motivated purely by self-interest; skepticism.

Democracy

A system of government by the whole population or all the eligible members of a state, typically through elected representatives.

Descendants

A person that is descended from a particular ancestor.

Detriment

The state of being harmed or damaged.

Discrimination

The unjust or prejudicial treatment of different categories of people, especially on the grounds of race, age, or sex.

Disdain

The feeling that someone or something is worthy of one's consideration or respect; contempt.

Disparities

Meaning to be of great difference.

Disproportionately

To an extent that is too large or too small in comparison with something else.

Domain

Meaning an area of speciality.

Economic Trends

An indicator that shows how a region or country is doing financially.

Emerge

To move out of or away from something and come into view.

Epithets
An adjective or descriptive phrase expressing a quality characteristic of the person or thing mentioned.

Epitomize
Meaning to be a perfect example of something.

Equality
The state of being equal, especially in status, rights, and opportunities.

Equity
The quality of being fair and impartial.

Exordium
The beginning or introductory part, especially of a discourse or treatise.

Exponentially
With reference to an increase which is more and more.

Extremism
A person who holds extreme or fanatical political or religious views, especially one who resorts to or advocates extreme action.

Extrinsic Motivation
Motivation encouraged by outside forces.

Financial Growth
An increase in one's financial resources due to the financial market.

Fluctuate
Rise and fall irregularly in number or amount.

Foundation
An underlying basis or principle.

Holistically
In a way that is characterized by comprehension of the parts of something as intimately interconnected and explicable only by reference to the whole.

Humanism
It is a belief that human needs and values are more important than religious and political beliefs.

Implement
Meaning to put into practice or to put into place.

Impoverished
Of a person or area made poor.

Inequality

Difference in size, degree, circumstances, or lack of equality.

Insurmountable

Meaning too great to be overcome.

Interest Rates

The proportion of a loan that is charged as interest to the borrower, typically expressed as an annual percentage of the loan outstanding.

Intrinsic Motivation

The act of being motivated without any external rewards or influences.

Isolate

Cause to be or remain alone or apart from others.

Liabilities

The state of being responsible for something, especially by law.

Marginalized

Of a person, group, or concept treated as insignificant or peripheral.

Mobility

The ability to move or be moved freely and easily.

Monetary
Relating to money or currency

Monopoly
The exclusive possession or control of the supply of or trade in a commodity or service.

Monumental
Meaning to be of great importance, extent, or size.

Municipal purposes
Meaning to include the use of land and the erection and use of buildings by or on behalf of the Council for the purpose of carrying out one or more municipal functions which may include the supply of essential protective, health, community, administrative, engineering, support or other purpose.

Natural Born Citizen
A person born within the United States regardless of the citizenship of their parents.

Networking
The action or process of interacting with others to exchange information and develop professional or social contacts.

Pandemic
An event in which a disease spreads across several countries and affects a large number of people.

Peregrination
A journey, especially a long or meandering one.

Peril
Serious and immediate danger.

Perplexing
Completely baffling; very confusing or puzzling.

Perseverance
Persistence in doing something despite difficulty or delay in achieving success.

Perspective
A particular attitude toward or way of regarding something; a point of view.

Pertinacious
Holding firmly to an opinion or a course of action.

Political System
A coordinated set of principles, laws, ideas, and procedures relating to a particular form of government itself.

Principles
A fundamental truth or proposition that serves as the foundation for a system of belief or behavior or for a chain of reasoning.

Productivity
The state or quality of producing something, especially in reference to the concepts of input and output.

Prophecy
A prediction.

Radicalism
The beliefs or actions of people who advocate thorough or complete political or social reform.

Regulations
A rule or directive made and maintained by an authority. The action or process of regulating or being regulated.

Replicate
Make an exact copy of; reproduce.

Reverential
Of the nature of, due to, or characterized by reverence.

Rhetoric
The art of effective or persuasive speaking or writing, especially the use of figures of speech and other compositional techniques. Meaning languages designed to have a persuasive or impressive effect on its audience, but often regarded as lacking in sincerity or meaningful content.

Spectrum
Used to classify something, or suggest that it can be classified, in terms of its position on a scale between two extreme or opposite points.

Sustain
To strengthen or support physically or mentally.

Systemic Racism
Institutionalized racism that is a form of racism that is embedded as normal practice within society or an organization. It can lead to such issues as discrimination in criminal justice, employment, housing, health care, political power, and education, among other issues.

Tenets
A principle or belief, especially one of the main principles
of a religion or philosophy.

Trife
Troublesome or causing trouble.

Visionary
Especially of a person thinking about or planning the
future with imagination or wisdom.

References

Baker, B.D., Farrie, D., Sciarra, D. (2018). Is school funding fair? A national report card. Retrieved December 31, 2020, from https://edlawcenter.org/assets/files/pdfs/publications/Is _School_Funding_Fair_7th_Editi.pdf

Baldwin, J. (1984). *Notes of a native son*. Boston: Beacon Press. 6th. Ed.

Bandura, A. (1973). *Aggression: A social learning analysis.* Prentice-Hall.

Bandura, A. (1986). *Social foundations of thought and action: A social cognitive theory.* Englewood Cliffs, NJ: Prentice Hall.386

Blair, C., & Diamond, A. (2008). Biological processes and intervention: The promotion of self-regulation as a means of preventing school failure. Development and Psychopathology Special Issue: Integrating Biological Measures into the Design and Evaluation of Preventive Interventions, 20, 899 –911.

Feinberg, M.E., Jones, D.E, Kan, M.L., & Goslin, M.C. (October 2010). *Journal of Family Psychology 24(5): 532-542.* DOI: 10.1037/a0020837

Gardner, H. (1999) *Intelligence reframed: multiple intelligences for the 21st century.* New York, NY: Basic Books.

Gregory, G., & Kuzmich, L. (2004). *Data driven differentiation in the standards-based classroom.* Thousand Oaks, Calif: Corwin Press.

Radcliffe, S. Oxford university Press: Essential quotations. (2017). https://DOI:10.1093/acref/9780191843730.001.0001

Roche, S. Editorial: Equity and equality in education. *Int Rev Educ 59, 1-5* (2013). https://doi.org/10.1007/s11159-013-9356-2

Triplett, A. (2018) "Incentive-Based Compensation Arrangements: An Examination of the Wells Fargo Scandal and the Need for Reform in Financial Institutions," University of Baltimore Law Review: Vol. 47 : Issue 2, Article6. Available at: https://scholarworks.law.ubalt.edu/ublr/vol47/iss2/6
Estimating Top Income and Wealth Shares: Sensitivity to Data and Methods
Jesse Bricker, Alice Henriques, Jacob Krimmel, John Sabelhaus, Federal Reserve Board Paper (PDF), October 2016

Wang, K., Chen, Y., Zhang, J., and Oudekerk, B.A. (2020). Indicators of School Crime and Safety: 2019 (NCES 2020-063/NCJ 254485). National Center for Education Statistics, U.S. Department of Education, and

Bureau of Justice Statistics, Office of Justice Programs, U.S. Department of Justice. Washington, DC.